Stevie Ray's Medium-Sized Book of Comedy

What We Laugh At ...and Why

by
Stevie Ray

Punchline
Publications

Punchline Publications
4600 Oakland Avenue South
Minneapolis, MN 55407-3536

Photography for front cover and About Author by:
Ann Marsden
Ann Marsden Photography, Minneapolis, MN

ISBN 0-9671786-0-6

Punchline Publications is a division of

Stevie Ray's Productions, a company

focused on entertainment and education; providing

performances, training, and related products and services.

Stevie Ray's *"Making it up as we go since 1989"*

This book is dedicated to:

My parents, Richard and Marcia Rentfrow. It is said that the acorn doesn't fall far from the oak tree, which I never understood because our yard had a maple. Thank you for passing along your wonderful sense of humor and for encouragement that allowed me to forge my own unique career path and avoid ever getting a real job.

Acknowledgments:

Brothers Mike and Dick and sister Ann, for laughing at my stuff, even when you didn't think it was funny. And for providing me with a lifetime of material, whether you liked it or not.

Pamela M. Vervair, co-founder of The Stevie Ray's Theatre Company and my business and artistic partner since 1989. A position that has required her to sit through my performances night after night, year after year. A feat deserving of sainthood. People need friends for inspiration and support, colleagues for professional fulfillment, and intimates for the occasional shoulder and ear. God gave me all that in you.

Manfred Haeusler, my first professional comedy partner. Thanks for letting me have the spotlight often enough to get addicted. Eugene Huddleston, the true Zen master of jazz comedy. You demonstrate passion and an unbending artistic integrity that serve as a guide for us all. Don Foster, one of the few people I know in this world with as much talent, intellect, and a true heart of gold . To the three of you, a good sword needs a thousand blows of the hammer to develop a sharp edge. The "Four Chinaski's" was my forge.

Dave & Joan Ellison for their editorial comments. Even when they conflicted with each other, which actually made the project more difficult.

Dr. Lee Morrow and Dr. Timothy Choy of Moorhead State University. Dr. Morrow for guiding me through my first academic venture into humor, and Dr. Choy for his academic guidance, support, and for planting the idea of this book into my head.

Amy Rost for her wonderful editorial help.

This book is also in memory of two students of the Stevie Ray's School of Improv who were taken from us much too soon.

Chris McCoy, in his late twenties decided that being a welder wasn't enough for him and started learning improvisation in 1991. As unfamiliar as performing was to him, whenever there was an opening in an improv troupe, he was first to audition. And after every audition, when I had to tell him he wasn't ready yet, he smiled and said, "I'll keep working, 'cause someday I'm going to be on stage." Were he still with us, I'm sure he would have made it.

Woody Leafer, a man who spent his life in the theatre, from Broadway to his own radio show in New Orleans interviewing the likes of Abbott and Costello and Rita Hayworth. When I asked him why, after a full career in theatre, he wanted to learn improvisation. He said, "I've always loved the theatre, but I hate to memorize lines." He started with me in 1995. I learned that he was 78 years old. I asked him why he had put 72 as his age on his registration card. He replied, "I didn't want people to think I was old." He was younger than any of us.

TABLE OF CONTENTS

Part III
MODERN COMEDY

Part IV
WHAT NOW?

Chapter 1

STEVIE RAY'S PYRAMID OF COMEDY

(Hey, if I called it the Introduction you wouldn't read it)

*"The most difficult character in comedy is the fool,
and he must be no fool who plays that part."*
Cervantes

What's so funny? Who do you think you're laughing at?
I'll bet you have no idea. Laughter is more vital to our lives
than most people realize. Our mental and physical health
depend on it. Laughter eases tense situations. It is a bonding
agent between people. It can cure sickness, promote
friendship, act as a barometer of culture, and can even help
change the course of society. Humor can indicate intelligence,
or the lack of it, as well as family background, ethnic heritage,
and social standing. Used with discretion, it can intrigue and
delight the opposite sex. Used indiscriminately, it can make
the opposite sex think you are an idiot (learned from personal
experience). Laughter can establish dominance over others, or
show support for a superior. It is the one means of

3

communication that can show both extreme confidence or uncontrolled nervousness.

Comedy is the most difficult and unpredictable style of performance. As easy as it is to inspire tears through an impelling dramatic performance, it is that much more difficult to inspire laughter. Comedy is at best a game of chance and it's success a gift of luck. Laughter can flow from an audience with ease, while minutes later the same group may be stone cold.

Humor is source of pride. Although people will readily admit, "I can't tell a joke very well," rare is it that you will hear someone say, "I have absolutely no sense of humor." Scan the "personals" section of a newspaper where people advertise for potential dates and *sense of humor* tops the list for desired qualities. The truth is, people aren't looking for someone with a *good* sense of humor, they want someone with a sense of humor that matches their own. That's generally how we define a good sense of humor, people who laugh at things we don't find funny are either sick, twisted, or stupid.

For some who make humor their profession, comedy goes beyond pride—it's a source of identity. This sentiment is reflected well in the movie *Punchline*. Tom Hanks' character, Steven Gold, says to Lila Krytseck, played by Sally Field, "*I'll say anything to a woman and not mean it. I'll say I love her, I'll say she's beautiful, I'll say she's sexy. I don't mess around with funny.*" It's that identity with comedy that started me on the road to my career, and my life's passion.

4

On a sunny Tuesday in May 1959, Marcia Rentfrow gave birth to Stephen, the second of her four children. When the baby was wrapped in a blanket and handed to the mother she beamed and said to her husband Richard, "Oh honey, maybe someday we'll have a *comedian* in the family." I've had that dream many times and I always wake up smiling. The smile fades when I realize it was only a dream and I remember my father's real words, "Comedy! What kind of a job are you going to get with that?" I heard that statement during a phone call home from college. I had called to announce that I was no longer interested in a regular job and had decided instead to create a new major, *Theory and Performance of Comedy.* No surprise that they never bragged to the neighbors about my new career choice. I count myself lucky though, the shock of my chosen profession hit my parents when I was young and they had time to recover before I got my first real gig. Still, it was quite a while before they stopped encouraging me to "get a real job so you'll have something to fall back on." Someday I would love to hear parents say to their child, "Better learn some acting in case that *doctor* thing doesn't work out for you!"

Actually, my becoming a comedian came as no surprise to anyone who knew me as a child. Little boys tend to be drawn to activities that will gain them attention, luckily mine happened to be non-destructive, unlike my younger brother who was fond of riding motorcycles off the roof of the house. Being a scrawny little tyke made humor more than an idle attraction in my case; it was necessary for survival. I had to have something to defuse dangerous situations on the

5

playground with Carl, the school bully. I think that's where comedians really learn to handle tough crowds. If you can talk your way out of eating dirt at the age of 6, drunk hecklers in a night club are a piece of cake.

And my family unwittingly set my life goal even as a toddler. Once a friend or relative discovers your penchant for humor, birthdays gifts are set for life. Once I uttered my first riddle, every Christmas and birthday afterwards was filled with presents for the "little funny guy." Riddle and joke books, anthologies of humor, records and tapes of Bill Cosby, Lily Tomlin, Flip Wilson, The Smothers Brothers, and quite a few very nice clown statuettes. God bless grandmothers who will sit and listen to you read every single riddle in the book and laugh, pretending that she hasn't heard them before. God bless parents who resist the urge to lock themselves in their room when you come home with 50 new jokes you heard at school. God bless brothers and sisters who tell you you're funnier than the guys on TV (okay, that last part never happened). So it's actually more their fault that I grew to crave the stage instead of an office. They still refuse to accept responsibility for it.

After meeting scores of other comedians in my work I discovered that the conditions that made me lean towards being funny are common to most comedians. It's not just the cliché "need for attention." It is something much deeper. The discovery of something at which we excel and that gives us a sense of identity, the same need that drives anyone to a chosen profession. If you're told at a young age, "Oh, you're such a good little woodworker," you're likely to watch a lot of those shows where they rebuild old houses (you know, the ones where two actors pretend they know what a Makita 3/8" cordless reversible drill is). If your family and teachers fawn over your crayon version of Van Gogh on the living room wall, you're set for a life of living in studio lofts, having paint under your fingernails, and not being able to pay bills. For me, the older brother was the smart one, the younger brother was the wild one, and the younger sister was good with animals. I had to find something that was mine, *all mine*.

My first real show was at a family talent show night at the YMCA in my hometown of Rochester, Minnesota. I was about nine years old. My parents decided my two brothers and I were going to perform a couple of funny skits (what professional comedians now call "sketches." The difference between a skit and a sketch is whether you're doing them around a campfire). I should preface by saying that my older brother, Dick* grew up to design weapons for a large defense company, and my younger brother, Mike* became an operator of the heart-lung machine used in open heart surgery. Nevertheless, these were the *comedians* I had to work with, not exactly Martin and Lewis. If you have to ask who Martin and Lewis are, stop reading, put the book back on the shelf, and go back to reruns of "Three's Company." Rehearsals did not go smoothly. Dick, being the oldest, didn't have any trouble playing his part with confidence and bravado.

Names have not been changed. They never cared about my privacy, so I don't care about theirs.

7

He was used to being in charge of our little trio, which is why we always got into so much trouble. His idea of playtime was to think of fun (i.e. destructive) things to do to the house, pet, plumbing, or local fire station, and convince Mike and I to do them. He was also clever enough to duck out before the authorities (parents) showed up, leaving Mike and me holding the bag.

But I digress. As I said, Dick was playing his part well, if a little stiffly. Mike was not into the performing arts, not then, not now. At the age of seven his idea of fun was...well...think of Dick and add the mind of Evel Kneivel. After a game involving a ten speed bike, a wooden ramp, a shoulder harness, and a parachute made out of a bedsheet he was never allowed to baby-sit sister Ann again. So Mike was not enjoying himself, and was not speaking his lines with the chutzpah that Mom wanted (no, we're not Jewish). Mom became frustrated, which made dad frustrated, which made mom more frustrated than she would have been if dad hadn't stood there being frustrated. This frustrated Mike, who stormed out of the living room to sulk in the kitchen. The whole thing blew when dad yelled at Mike, "You get in here. You're going to do this skit and be funny dammit!" The irony was not lost on me even then. I had a feeling comedy was for me when, after all this, I still thought it would be fun.

The big night came and we waited at our table as the other families performed. A father and his three-year-old boy performed a balancing act with the boy standing on his father's upstretched hands as the dad lay on the ground. They got polite

8

applause. A twelve-year-old girl sang a folk song while her mother played piano. They got polite applause. A family of four sang an a capella Christmas song that the mother had obviously selected without consideration of the father's vocal range. More polite applause. As I looked around I saw the expressions on people's faces that said, "Oh, he's cute!" "What a sweet little girl." At the tender age of nine, before ever stepping foot on stage, I discovered something. **I did not want** *polite* **applause**. Being funny in our skits was too important to me to allow myself to be patronized by some grown-up's insincerity. I wanted laughs. Big, hearty, hold-your-stomach, this-kid-should-be-in-Vegas **laughs**.

I looked at my brothers as they quietly watched the other acts. They weren't enjoying themselves. You never enjoy yourself when your turn is coming up. All you can do is sit and think, "I hope I don't suck as bad as that guy." So I prayed. I prayed that we would remember our lines. I prayed that Dick wouldn't think the whole thing was stupid and walk off the stage. I prayed that Mike wouldn't set anything on fire. I prayed the audience would laugh.

Then came our turn. Our skit had me cast as the editor of a newspaper and my brothers as reporters. They would run in screaming, "Stop the presses, stop the presses!" I would ask them what news they had. They would tell me of some incredible disaster. I would ask when it happened and they would say one or two days ago. I would yell at them and throw them out of my office saying, "I want fresh news, and only fresh news!" This went on until Mike burst in to tell me of a

9

flash flood. "When?" I asked. "Right now!" he replied, and threw a glass of water in my face, ending the skit.

At that moment I heard something for the first time that would set my life in motion forever, an audience laughing. The entire room was on the floor. And it wasn't a room full of my dorky schoolmates laughing at Carl Olson making fart noises with his arm (I hated that guy, and that armpit thing). These were *adults*. In my short life on the earth I had never heard a sweeter sound. I stood there with my heart pounding so loud I could hardly hear them applaud. I don't remember a single act for the rest of the show. After that laughter and applause nothing else registered for the rest of the night. During the reception after the show friends of my parents told them I had a natural talent for humor. One man said to my father, "That kid's got great comic timing."

That was all I needed. Throughout grade school I focused not on what was on the chalk board, but what was on my classmates desks and how they could be made funny. In high school I hit every talent show with a comedy routine borrowed (stolen) from some comedy great. By the time I finished college I had soaked up routines by Jonathan Winters, George Carlin, Red Skelton, Flip Wilson, Richard Pryor, Steve Martin, Bob Newhart, and Lily Tomlin. I had watched hours of "The Jerry Lewis Show," "The Smothers Brothers," "The Munsters," "Tom & Jerry," "Bugs Bunny," "I Dream of Jeannie," "I Love Lucy," "The Honeymooners," "Laugh-In," "The Dick Van Dyke Show," "Saturday Night Live," "Gilligan's Island," "The Andy Griffith Show," "Monty Python's Flying Circus," and

"Fawlty Towers." And I memorized every word of my hero of then and now, Bill Cosby. I studied classic and modern theories of comedy, the psychology of laughter, and the basis of humor in society. I expanded my learning beyond a solo act and performed with a partner in showcases and local night clubs. I began learning sketch comedy and troupe improvisation.

After college I worked at comedy clubs as everything from box office clerk to managing director. I spent five years at Dudley Riggs' Brave New Workshop comedy theatre in Minneapolis as a technician, actor, writer, and improvisation teacher. The Brave New Workshop is a satirical sketch-revue theatre older than Chicago's The Second City. I toured the country as a stand-up comedian, working clubs from Sioux Falls to San Francisco. And I continued to study; books by psychologists, sociologist, theatre critics, comedians, and philosophers. All of whom tried to explain the meaning of things comic.

Through these volumes I relearned something I had always known, that humor is more than an amusing pastime. As I grew as a comedic performer and teacher I also grew in my understanding of what makes people laugh. I learned that beyond the stage, creating comedy in the spontaneous atmosphere of everyday life is not nearly as difficult. Since it is one of our most treasured forms of communication we seek it out constantly.

In a research project, Robert Provine, a professor of psychology at the University of Maryland Baltimore County, discovered that laughter during normal conversation occurs more from friendly banter than from formal and structured attempts at humor. Laughter in social settings is more a reaction of playfulness than from what would be considered comedy performance. So, laughter in everyday life is more accidental that planned.

Laughter is one of the few universal expressions in the world. No matter how great the differences between races and cultures, there is laughter in all of us, and surprisingly, people around the world laugh at generally the same things. Children from all cultures laugh when playing tag, professional comedians the world over poke fun at important political and social figures, and little boys everywhere hide in their own version of a tree house to tell a dirty joke.

Laughter is the one form of communication that truly separates us from animals (aside from professional wrestling and talk shows). This is true with one notable exception. Chimpanzees and other apes have their own form of laugh that comes during physical play or from tickling. It is interesting to note that ape laughter differs from our own in its physical manifestation. When humans laugh they let out a series of short sounds, "Ha ha ha" as they exhale. The whole laugh takes as long as our breath lasts, then we inhale and start another series of laughs. This is the same pattern we use when we speak, letting out a series of words until our breath runs out. Chimpanzees laugh with a short "ah" sound that is made as the chimp alternately inhales and exhales. This creates laugh sounds that are shorter and more clipped than in humans. The creation of a "ha" sound would be difficult and even painful if a human tried to inhale to say it, but it is completely natural for apes. Scholars who work with apes believe it is this inhale/exhale method of creating clipped sounds that prevents apes from speaking. Some chimps have been taught to say monosyllabic words like "cup" or "go," but sustained speech is impossible with the breathing limitation. Also of note is that apes only laugh when engaged in a physical activity, such as tickling, or chasing, or wrestling. This points to their inability to intellectually discern other types of comedy, which we will discuss in this book.

Doctors have begun to see not only the benefit, but the medical necessity for laughter. Researchers have discovered that laughter produces much-needed hormones and immuno-chemicals that ensure good physical and mental health. Companies and corporations are hiring laughter and humor consultants to help create a more positive work environment using laughter. Conventions focusing on humor are being sponsored nationwide by professionals in the fields of psychology, sociology, medicine, and interpersonal communications.

With our age-old love of comedy and our new-found interest in the science of laughter, the day may actually come when parents wish for a new *comedian* in the family when a child is born. With the positive effect comedians have on those around them, wouldn't it make sense to revere those who make us laugh more than people who do infommercials on TV The time is soon coming when comedy will hold a much higher place in society than it does now.

Some would say the rise in status of comedy is due to the "comedy boom" of the 80s, when the nation went from a handful of comedy clubs located in major cities, to hundreds of clubs across the country. It seemed that overnight you could skip traveling to New York or Los Angeles for a night of live comedy, every hotel and fast food joint had "Comedy Night." Bars and nightclubs replaced "Wet T-Shirt Night" with "Amateur Comedy Hour" (I hated when they did that). Television became so littered with comedy shows you couldn't turn on the set without seeing someone in front of a brick wall with a microphone and a lousy suit. The thirst for comedy was so huge that *Comedy Central* was born, a station devoted entirely to comedy programming. Comedians today talk about the comedy boom like old-timers talking about the days when gasoline was a nickel. Actually, there was no comedy boom in the 80s, there was a *stand-up* comedy boom, and yes there is a difference. Comedy itself has never lost its appeal. It doesn't cycle up and down like the stock market; it merely changes its form to fit the times and to appeal to our fickle nature.

The stand-up comedy we enjoy today is simply the current incarnation of a substance we have needed and enjoyed since we first developed language. We have always loved comedy because we have always needed laughter to survive. It is only recently that we have begun to realize it's importance as more than a pleasant diversion.

Yet, for all our love and need of comedy, most people don't really understand it. Few can say why some people laugh at the Three Stooges and others think the Stooges are just three stupid men hitting each other. Ask the person on the street what makes them laugh, and they'll usually give you the name of a favorite comedian or TV show. Ask them why they laugh and they'll say, "'Cause it's funny." Press them for what make something or someone funny and they won't have a clue. Many comedians and comedy performers are baffled as to why a joke or routine has one audience rolling in the isles and another sitting like Mount Rushmore. Unable to discern *why* a joke works, performers are left to play a game of trial and error, hoping that time and experience will develop in them an instinct that will carry them past the no-laugh landmines of comedy. With this in mind, it is no wonder the profession is so difficult and uncertain.

To ask why people laugh is to ask why people eat. The answer to either is just as complex. Some people eat because they know it is healthy for them; others eat as a reaction to stress. For some, eating is the focus of their lives. They spend many hours and dollars searching for new eating experiences and exotic tastes. Eating can also be a response to psychological disorders, the symptom of deep emotional pain that causes the eater to use food as a crutch. Even though eating is a necessity and a person must eat to stay alive, the *motivation* to eat may be healthy or dysfunctional.

Laughter is no different than other physical needs. Laughter is as much a reaction as it is a choice. It can be a healthy expression of joy, or an instrument of cruelty. It can enhance life by bringing happiness to others, or it can display nervousness and discomfort. It can express the exultation of someone who is self-actualized and fulfilled, or it can expose cynicism and bitterness. To say that we laugh for any one reason is as ridiculous as saying that we eat only to stay alive. As my father used to say, *Some people eat to live, some live to eat.* I am fortunate to live for laughter.

There are many reasons why we laugh, and there are many sources of laughter. Philosophers have tried for centuries to nail down the true source of laughter, Aristotle thought it was psychological. Plato thought it was social; Freud thought it was psychological and sexual (no big surprise there). Sometimes comedy is funny de jure, (topical humor, comedy of the day, and sometimes it is funny de facto (humor in actuality, funny to all people all the time). Humor *in actuality* is the focus of this book.

One thing common to people everywhere is the progression of their *comedic maturity.* When we experience our very first laugh as an infant, it is at a specific type of humor, a simple and repetitive form of comedy. This is because our brains aren't developed enough to understand complex thinking and the humor that accompanies it. As we grow older and gain experience, our knowledge of the world broadens, allowing us to enjoy a wider variety of humor. I have divided comedy into seven levels: *Physical Comedy, Obscenity and Profanity, Storyline, Language, Imitation, Character Contradiction,* and *Satire.* The list starts at the lowest level of comedy, that which requires the least intellect to understand, and progresses to the highest. So, the level of understanding and intellectual experience must be high in order for the individual to find humor in higher forms of comedy.

For this reason, the terms *high comedy* and *low comedy* are used. That is not to say that those who enjoy "low" forms of humor have a lower IQ than others; slapstick is enjoyed by many very intelligent people. It merely means that low comedy requires little intellect for laughter to occur. The more intellect a person has, the broader range of comedy experiences can be enjoyed. The categories in *Stevie Ray's Pyramid of Comedy* each reflect a unique area of humor. Each level represents a type of humor that incites laughter for its own specific reason. I call it a pyramid because the lower levels of comedy can be understood by broader sections of society.

Some people voice a preference for specific types of comedy—"I like comics, but I don't like plays," "I can't laugh at dirty jokes, but I love those cute comic strips." The nature of comedy is that *it is* or *it occurs*, and we don't really choose when or where we laugh. The levels of humor discussed here are inherent to all comedy and to all types of laughter. They are true for comedy that exists on the stage, the page, at home, or at roam (God I hate it when people rhyme like that).

The nature and conditions of comedy are the same whether you are watching a play, a stand-up routine, or your father fight with the garden hose. The reasons for your laughter are the same as everyone esle. At least in laughter, we are all the same.

17

Part I
COMEDY DISSECTED

Chapter 2
PHYSICAL COMEDY

"Comedy is tragedy that happens to someone else."
Unknown

Moe: *"Why you lamebrain, I'll moidah ya"*
POINK! (Poke in the eye)
Curly: *"Ow Ow Ow Ow Ow"*

Decades ago, when a man named Roark Bradford was working as a reporter for a newspaper, he was assigned to interview the great screen comedian, Ben Turpin. Bradford held the interview in the wings of the vaudeville theatre where Turpin was playing. Bradford asked him, "What is the essence of comedy?" Turpin replied, "I'll show you." He walked on stage, using many grand gestures and grimaces, getting no response from the audience. Turpin walked back to Bradford and said, "Now watch again." He ran on stage and fell flatly on his behind, to the uproarious laughter of the audience. Turpin returned to the reporter and said, "That is the essence of comedy."

The sketch I performed as a child at the YMCA had me getting a glass of water thrown in my face. Ordinarily, as a timid little eight year old, I tried to avoid public attention and humiliation, but I couldn't wait for the end of that sketch because I knew that was where the laugh would be. It was great for a child like to me to see the adults laughing just as hard as the kids, but it surprised me to see the grown-ups laughing at something so juvenile. I learned then that the love of good slapstick never goes away.

Since intellectual ability is the determining factor in the appreciation of comedy, physical humor is the lowest level. With physical humor (peek-a-boo games with a child, a cartoon character falling off a cliff, a clown honking his nose) there is no intellect needed to understand the joke because there is no actual joke. The laughter is generated from surprise and a playful attitude. As we get older and find humor in higher levels of comedy, we sometimes have to think to understand the references and meaning within the joke. We have to work a little harder upstairs in the brain, and this slows down the laugh. A minute pause occurs before the joke sinks in and the humor is revealed.

Even as adults however, when we see physical comedy we immediately explode into laughter. The physical misfortune of others affects a very basic part of the human psyche. It inspires an immediate response from the viewer. Think back to the last time that, without even thinking, you laughed at someone poking themselves in the eye, or slipping on an icy sidewalk. After the initial laugh you realized that the person could have been hurt. Perhaps you were embarrassed, and found yourself apologizing for laughing. Why would civilized human beings find pleasure in someone else's misfortune? What causes the initial response of laughter before the concern for well-being sets in?

Henri Bergson, a French philosopher from the early 1900s, created a theory about comedy called "the mechanical encrusted upon the living." He believed that anytime a person took on the characteristics of a machine, that image would be humorous and the result would be laughter. He believed that the source of humor was the appearance that the person was completely out of control of their own situation. We can see how some situations make a person look machine-like and out of control.

In one episode of the TV situation comedy, "Cheers," the character of Cliff Clavin has arranged to meet a woman for a date on the steps of the bar at 8 o'clock. The appointed hour comes and goes with no woman in sight. With each passing hour Cliff gets more and more nervous. When she finally arrives we learn that she was late because she was just as nervous about meeting Cliff. They gaze into each other's eyes and become transfixed. They stand motionless for so long that the bar owner, Sam Malone finally goes over to the jukebox, puts in a coin, and selects a romantic song. Standing eight feet apart, Cliff and the woman don't move. Sam walks over and whispers into Cliff's ear. As he begins to walk away he notices that they are still frozen. He pauses, then walks over to the woman and positions her arms in the air as if she were dancing cheek-to-cheek. He does the same to Cliff, stands behind him and, planting his hands on Cliff's rear, pushes him into the frozen arms of his date. Thinking he has completed his task, he begins to walk away. Taking a couple of steps he sees that they still haven't moved. He reaches over to Cliff's shoulder and, like one would start a rocking toy, nudges them. They start to rock back and forth and gradually begin to dance.

The above scene is a perfect example of Bergson's theory that people are humorous when they give the impression of being mechanical. Cliff and his date looked and acted like mannequins, and Sam's positioning of their arms confirmed the appearance. Every action reinforced the non-living facade, right up to the nudge that set the toys in motion.

Bergson has another theory, the "Jack-in-the-box" theory, that is an extension of "the mechanical encrusted upon the living." The delight a child finds in a Jack-in-the-box game revolves around the fact that no matter how many times Jack's head is pushed back into the box, he pops up that same way every time, completely out of control of the situation. Imagine a man walking by an empty swing. He bumps into the swing accidentally and gets angry. He pushes the swing away forcefully and turns away from it. The swing returns, hitting the man in the head and knocking him down. As he gets up, the swing returns, knocking him down again, and again, and again. Each time he is knocked down, getting up becomes more difficult and his actions more and more exaggerated. He seems unable to perform the simplest remedy, to move aside and let the swing by. The whole scene is very machine-like, and funny. Speed up the action to look like the old hand-operated black-and-white movies, and it is hilarious. In situations like this, people laugh even if they think they shouldn't. My mother once let out a laugh when a stranger fell flat on his butt while trying to ice skate. After a quick chuckle she said, "Oh, I shouldn't laugh!" Physical humor connects to a basal part of our thinking, so our laugh is much less under our control than if we were to hear a funny story or joke. If we listen to a friend tell a joke, we must put ourselves in the mood to laugh in order to enjoy it—not always so with physical humor.

Physical humor is also based on what Bergson called "the appearance of inelasticity." Since humans are endowed with the ability to adapt to their surroundings (our "elasticity"), any display of physical inability contradicts our natural adaptability. This brings a person to a base level of the comic. Take for instance the opening credits of the Dick Van Dyke Show. As the introduction music plays, Van Dyke's character, Rob Petri, comes home from work and is surprised to see his co-workers Sally Rogers and Buddy Surrell sitting in his living room. As he moves to greet them he falls over an ottoman and does a perfect shoulder-roll fall. At the opening of every single episode he falls over the ottoman, and we laugh every time. Rob can not seem to control his actions—he is completely inelastic. The fact that the intro music is playing and there is no dialogue completes the look of a live Jack-in-the-box.

Physical comedy is also funny when it contrasts a base issue with a moral or ethereal one. If a speaker was giving a moving political speech, and the entire audience was enthralled at his wisdom and insight, and just at the climax of his speech, he farted, the audience would be on the floor. Physical humor brings high-minded issues immediately to a common level because any physical act of the body instantly reminds us of our humanity. The contrast of high-minded thinking and common humanity causes laughter. It also appeals to our need to establish our sense of personal power. If the speaker is talking about a subject of great philosophical or social importance, we feel small and powerless in its grandeur. A quick fart reminds us that he is just as vulnerable as we.

Physical humor brings everyone down to the same level. Many amateur speakers who experience stage-fright are told to imagine the audience in their underwear. Their fear is erased because they have used the qualities of physical humor to bring the audience they fear down to their own level. Imagine how much less you would fear your boss if, just before going into a tense meeting, you were to imagine him or her sitting on the toilet...pants down around the ankles...with no toilet paper on the roll.

Sigmund Freud had some interesting ideas about physical humor. Some remember Freud only as the Father of Psychoanalysis and creator of the Oedipus Complex. Many do not realize that he also studied the psychology of humor, becoming interested in its connection to the mind after reading the theories on humor of the Munich professor, Theodore

Lipps. In 1905 Freud published a book that was his greatest departure from the field of psychoanalysis, Jokes and Their Relation to the Unconscious. Freud believed that man achieves physical comedy by displaying an exaggerated amount of energy for a simple task. Man is proud of his ability to overcome his surroundings, and strives to decrease the amount of effort needed for everyday tasks. This is why we create so many machines to do our work for us. The need to do as little work as possible is the human characteristic relied upon heavily by the creators of such gadgets as the Potato Slicer, the One-Step Button Mender, and the Automatic Envelope-and-Stamp-Licker. We think quite highly of ourselves for being able to make machines to most of our work, so if a person displays too much effort for a simple task we find it funny. Circus clowns use this principal regularly, flailing their arms and feet wildly just to get in and out of a chair. We laugh at the clown because he is incapable of using the mental and physical abilities we all possess.

Comedy also appeals to the malice in each of us and the desire to see others fail. In many ways comedy is criticism, and much of its material is centered around human imperfection. When we laugh at the person who fell on the ice, we are actually criticizing him or her for not being a more capable human being. Comedy, however, is a happy form of criticism, demonstrating that man is able to accept his limitations with good humor. Physical comedy shows that our individual limitations are common in everyone, making them easier to accept. By displaying them openly and in a humorous setting, all of our physical limitations are diminished.

In some cases physical comedy can be the opposite of ridicule or criticism. It can be the verbal applause for physical agility. In the case of live performance, it is the *aliveness* of physical comedy that makes us love the theatre. The use of wild, energetic physical movements gives people a sense of triumph over the world. The rhythm and excitement of physical comedy gives the audience a sense of exhilaration, this sense of triumph breaks out in laughter. In this way, physical comedy is a celebration of life.

Physical comedy can also be funny because it visually represents humanity's constant battle against machine. The battles of man vs. machine, and man vs. nature are comical because we know that man is always going to lose, at least in a comedy setting. In drama, man is usually victorious over machines. In the movie <u>Terminator</u>, a futuristic world has man warring with robots. In the movie, a robot played by Arnold Schwartzenegger is sent back in time to the present to kill a boy who would eventually grow up to be one of their greatest enemies. A man from the future also comes back in time to try to save the boy from the robot. The plot is similar in the sequel, <u>Terminator II</u>, and the result is the same, man wins. In a real-life depiction of the world, people would not be happy with a story that showed the demise of humanity. So, although there are a number of books and movies with man's defeat at the conclusion, the majority of man versus machine stories end with us winning.

In comedy, however, we allow ourselves to see the opposite. The threat is not as real if our mood is lighter, we can accept defeat in the name of fun. In fact, because it's comedy we actually expect defeat. So, we build up an expectation of failure, and see it played out in front of us. We just love being right! The various manners in which the fight is lost can add even more comic potential to a scene. There are the deadpan expressions of Stan Laurel and Oliver Hardy as a car slowly collapses beneath them. Their faces literally say, "What's the point of fighting it? We're going to lose anyway." There is the ever-optimistic attitude of Charlie Chaplin as he is tossed from a restaurant for not paying the bill, urging us to cheer for the Little Tramp to go back and try again, even though we know he will probably get tossed out again. In the movie *Arthur*, Dudley Moore's character Arthur Bach, gets drunk and falls down a steep hill behind his house. As soon as he hits the bottom the phone rings on his terrace and he begins frantically climbing back up the hill. Everyone in the audience knows he won't make it in time. The harder he tries to hurry up the hill the harder it becomes and the more persistent the phone rings. It actually seems as if the hill is against Arthur, as each branch he grabs for support tears loose from the ground and he tumbles back to the bottom. Of course, he finally climbs the hill and picks up the phone just in time to hear the dial tone. The scene has the same comic quality as the frantic struggling of black-and-white film star Harold Lloyd as he tries to hang on to the face of a huge clock, the hands of the clock swinging, falling, and refusing to cooperate.

An important aspect of physical humor relates to the clock and the branches on the hill "refusing" to cooperate, that of the *humanness of an object*. An object is funny if it contains human characteristics. Objects that don't perform the task for which they were designed seem stubborn, uncooperative, or mischievous. Listen to a man working on a car trying to get it to start: "Come on you son-of-a..." "Please girl, come on!" Comedy takes advantage of our habit of endowing objects with human characteristics. This pattern extends to animals as well. We all know pets who are funny because they remind us of people we know. The attitude of an object or animal may be either hostile, such as a vacuum cleaner angrily chasing a man around the room, or entirely impersonal, such as a dog that passively sits as its owner tries in vain to lift him from the couch. Either way the attitude is human.

There is another element of physical comedy, the idea of *poetic metaphor*. This means that the physical object actually represents a higher idea. The man struggling against a lawn chair could signify that God is punishing him for trying to snooze instead of doing his yard work. This is more apt to be the case in situations where the character is having trouble with an object and we as the audience are aware that the person is up to no good. A bank robber may struggle with an angry safe door; a scheming little girl must navigate through a maze of loud toys to sneak out of the house instead of doing her chores. In each case, we know they are trying to get away with something, and the objects stand in their way. It is even more funny if, once they are caught, they actually become angry at the object for exposing them. We laugh and identify with the object, making an ally of something inanimate.

One reason physical comedy causes laughter is that it breaks routine. When we see someone walking down the street, we expect that they will continue walking until they are out of sight. If they fall over a trash barrel on the sidewalk, we laugh because of the surprise—the routine we expected was broken. So physical comedy also plays upon people's natural tendency to form expectations. John Greig, in The Psychology of Laughter and Comedy, says that all physical comedy is related to sex (what do you know, Freud has company). He believed that the violence associated with physical comedy invokes an ambivalent love-hate response.

Because many forms of violence are unconsciously associated with sexual acts, physical humor helps us release our inner feelings of sexual aggression. A look at comedies that involve man/woman relationships illustrates this point. On the television show, "Cheers," the characters, Diane Chambers and Sam Malone were simultaneously attracted and repulsed by each other. As audience members we could see through their insults because we knew that each had the hots for the other. In one scene their argument turns physical, and Diane grabs Sam's nose as he grabs her ear. Neither will let go and the stand-off becomes more and more painful with each minute. As Sam tightens his grip on Diane's ear she twists his nose. They both wince and groan in pain, but neither will let go. We laugh because not only do they seem unable to control their situation, but because we know they really want to grab a different part of the other's body.

Sometimes the sexual overtones aren't quite so hidden. In the movie, *Broadway Danny Rose,* Woody Allen's character, Danny Rose, finds himself in trouble with the mob and is left tied up with a female acquaintance, Tina Vitale, played by Mia Farrow. The scene is immediately sexual because they are tied together with Danny laying on his back on a table and Tina face down on top of him. The scene gets even more sexually amusing when Danny says that he used to represent an escape artist, "Shandar" (great name) who escaped from ropes during his act by wriggling his body. So Danny and Tina stand up, tied face to face, and start wriggling. Woody Allen's dialogue for the two is wonderful:

Danny:...*So, so are you ready? Ready?*

Tina: *Yeah.*

Danny: *All right now, start to wriggle. That's right. Wriggle. Yeah, see what I mean? That's it, that's a girl. Thrust, wriggle. That's it.*

Tina: *Hey, I'm wriggling.*

Danny: *That's it. Keep wrig...Oh, keep wriggling. That's very important. Are you wriggling?*

Tina: *Uh huh.*

Danny: *Oh, whooo.*

Tina: *I'm wriggling.*

Danny: *That's good. That's good wriggling.*

Tina: *I don't want to...overwriggle*

Danny: *No...no, but it's nice wriggling. That's it. The ropes are starting to get loose. Come on, it's happening, come on, my hand's getting free. Keep wriggling. Don't stop now. Oh, I got it, I got it.*

Tina: *Yeah?*

Danny: *I got it, yeah, yeah. Hold on. I got it. I got it.*

Tina: *Yes?*

Danny: *Yeah, yeah.*

Tina: *Oh...(panting) Great.*

Danny: *(struggling with ropes) Now, come on, keep wriggling, KEEP WRIGGLING darling.*

People have a natural tendency to seek pleasure, so physical comedy is a way of associating a bad stimulus, pain, with a good stimulus, laughter. Freud believed that since sex is an immediate form of pleasure, and associating physical comedy with sex makes the comedy more pleasurable. Freud also mentioned sexual aggression as a reason for humor, but mainly in the area of vulgarity, which will be discussed in the next chapter.

There are, of course, cases where physical mishap is not funny. You learned this the first time your mother scolded you for laughing at a person in a wheelchair, but beyond the social limitations placed on us there are psychological limitations as well. A deformity may only become comic if it is one that a normal person can successfully imitate, and one that does not represent too much of a threat to our sensibilities. Notice how people will imitate peculiar walks and voices and make you laugh. However, a gross deformity, like someone with a severe skin condition, is not imitatable, and physical humor is not possible. Also, many people would feel such pity for this person that laughter is suppressed. People may still make fun of the inflicted person by telling jokes at their expense, but the humor then becomes linguistic, not physical.

The question of poor taste is always an issue when the target of humor is someone who is disabled or afflicted with an illness. For many, this type of humor is a means of dealing with their own fear of death and disease, for others it is an affirmation of their own power. Those who admonish the joke teller for showing poor taste are met with "Come on, where's your sense of humor?" I suspect the question of taste in comedy will forever be a source of tension among people.

There are so many different theories about physical comedy one might wonder what its true basis is. In truth, a form of humor such as physical comedy cannot come from a single source. Comedy that forms the base of the pyramid will spring from many different parts of the brain. Our need for laughter and our instinct for finding a place in society causes us to develop a myriad of motivations for comedy. As infants and young children we see the world with a narrow view, and our appreciation of comedy reflects our self-centered frame of mind. As we mature and learn to appreciate new forms of humor, we don't replace physical comedy as a means of laughter - we add to it. As we add to our comedy storeroom we will add new ways to enjoy old styles, so when we reach adulthood physical comedy will entertain us for many different reasons, just as it did when we were children. Whether it is to ridicule someone's ineptness, to reward physical skill, to discover humanness in objects or machine-ness in people, or simply to register surprise, just give me a banana peel and an innocent bystander and I'm happy.

Chapter 3
OBSCENITY AND PROFANITY

*Congress shall make no law respecting an establishment of religion, or prohibiting the free exercise thereof; **or abridging the freedom of speech**, or of the press;...*
1st Amendment to the Constitution
Ratified: December 15, 1791

"I don't ever want to hear that word out of your mouth again!"
Marcia "Mom" Rentfrow
Ratified: August 12, 1963

Warning: The following chapter contains language that may offend younger or sensitive readers.
Parental discretion is advised.

Welcome to the most controversial area of comedy. The use of socially unacceptable language, gestures, and subject matter is to some, hilarious, and to others, disgusting. Lenny Bruce went to jail for it, George Carlin became famous for it, and most comedians have at one time or another, resorted to it for a quick laugh. Each year the guardians of public sensibility, in the form of television network censors, release a list of new words that are deemed acceptable for use on TV. This is done at the annual Professional Comedians Association convention. After the announcement is made, hundreds of veteran and aspiring comedians frantically review their acts to see how much further they can push the limits of good taste before a "beep" is put in place of the punchline.

It is an odd circumstance and a telling statement about humanity that all profanity or obscenity is a slang reference to bodily functions. Obscenity deals almost exclusively with the sexual and excretory parts of the body. *Urinate* becomes *pee, intercourse* becomes *screw,* and *defecate* becomes *shit.* A clinical term is available for each slang word, but people love variety, and sometimes clinical phraseology just doesn't carry enough oomph. To varying degrees, our social inhibitions prohibit us from using a profane word, and yet the clinical term seems too formal for a casual conversation. So the nightclub, with its dark lighting and atmosphere of anonymity, is the ideal place for breaking the social taboo of language and letting loose with a round of vulgarisms.

Obscenity has remained essentially the same throughout history. In fact, it is surprising how the obscene language of Greek Old Comedies parallels that of today. The Greek playwright, Aristophanes, filled his plays with *dick, prick*, and *screw.* He often had actors costumed with a huge phallus strapped on the waist. Much laughter was garnered by having the sexually frustrated actor actually address the simulated body part, "Oh good friend, when will we see satisfaction?" Our fascination with our bodies has changed little over time.

There are some cultural differences in the way slang is used, for instance Old Greek plays contain no references to urination, whereas today we have *piss, tinkle, wizz, leak,* and *pee.* Some cultures view public discussion of bodily acts as taboo and other cultures view it as normal. In cultures where open discussion of bodily functions is normal, few slang terms for the functions exist, except with children. It seems that in most cultures children find more pleasure in referring to bodily functions than do adults. In cultures where the parents frown on such discussion the delight the children have in breaking the taboo is even greater.

Why do we laugh at profanity? Sigmund Freud attributed the use of profanity to the unconscious mind. He reasoned that obscenity is a form of verbal exhibitionism. The user bares him or herself in front of the audience by the use of suggestive language. This causes anxiety on the part of the audience because such behavior is not normally acceptable. When the suggestive language leads to a pleasant joke instead of an aggressive attack, we are relieved of the tension and it escapes us through laughter. Freud believed we laugh at profanity as a release of anxiety, a form of mental safety valve. This type of laughter stems from feelings we had as children, but suppressed as we became adults. As adults we rarely have the opportunity to experience simple joy, so we sub-consciously seek it out, and profanity allows us to instantly recall the joy we had as children. Freud calls these "primary joys," the simple pleasures that are released by the use of low forms of comedy such as profanity.

This is a rather simplified view of why laughter is the product of obscene language. It does not take into account why one situation where profanity is used will cause laughter and another scorn. If we take for granted that the attitude of both the user of profanity and the listener are light-hearted, we can suppose that the levity of the moment allows them the freedom to suspend moral and social restrictions, and laugh at language which, in another situation, they would find repulsive.

Profanity carries so much more emotion than its clinical term counterpart that it becomes an effective tool for communicating ideas rather than information. This is important, since comedy is more reliant on emotion than facts. In comedy, the *intent* is just as important as the word itself. As opposed to clinical terms, obscene words have their own attitude; from silly *"I have to go doodily doo,"* to harsh *"I said fuck off."* Because of the strong emotion attached to it, obscenity becomes either a sword to attack, or a feather to tickle.

Comedy is often used as a means to challenge authority, and obscenity is the quickest means to achieve this. One of the causes of laughter in general is the breaking of the norm, an interruption in the normal order of events. Breaking the normal order of events sends the message to the audience that the speaker is not intimidated by authority, and will do things as he or she pleases. The laughter is stronger when the breach of order involves a forbidden subject. Graphic discussions about sex remain one of the few forbidden subjects in public conversation. So obscenity and it's reference to sexual acts is a quick and easy way to induce laughter by delivering surprise as well as dealing with forbidden subject matter. Laughter at obscenity, and the use of profanity by the comedian, becomes a form of rebellion. It is a chance to laugh at the very inhibitions we perpetuate in our own society. When a dirty joke is told in public, the listener feels simultaneously aroused and embarrassed. In some cases the basis of laughter is the contrast of two opposing emotions, thus producing a nervous laugh. The speaker feels a sense of freedom and power. Some comedians go so far as to say, "I know you're not supposed to talk about this stuff, but to hell with it. I'm saying it anyway!"

Obscenity seems to satisfy the basic urge of humans. One very strong urge is the natural curiosity men and women have toward each other. Take, for example, a scene from David Mamet's play, *Sexual Perversity in Chicago.*

Danny: So tell me.
Deb: What?
Danny: Everything. Tell me the truth about everything. Menstruation. I know you're holding out on me.
Deb: It would be hard on me if it got out. It's under our conscious control.
Danny: I knew it.
Deb: We just do it to drive you crazy with the mess.
Danny: I just knew it...
Deb: Now you tell me some.
Danny: Name it.
Deb: What does it feel like to have a penis?
Danny: Strange. Very strange and wonderful.

Deb: Do you miss having tits?

This popular play was later adapted as a movie, *About Last Night,* starring James Belushi, Rob Lowe, and Demi Moore. Notice how Mamet used a combination of clinical terminology and slang in the conversation. Part of the fun of the scene is to see the questions we all had as children, but were never allowed to discuss "in mixed company" being exposed in adult conversation.

Talented performers are able to use innuendo to achieve some of the same effects as obscenity, that of relating to sexual situations, without breaking social taboos or making the audience feel uncomfortable. See how Jonathan Winters skirts around the obvious in his routine, "Necking in a '38 Ford." This selection is from an album that was recorded live at Randy Sparks' Ledbetters Club in Los Angeles. Winters knew his audience was going to be a younger, college-age crowd. Knowing that their minds would be centered around sex and cars, he attempted to deal with their interests without going below the belt. Winters always said, "Better to be suggestive, even better to be realistic."

I had a '38 Ford. which is now a collector's item. ... you can be sitting in the car just the two of you, you know, and listening to the radio. That's usually the guys approach, get a little music, a little atmosphere going. Man, you're necking up a storm. ...About two or three hours, and then just about the time you think you're home free. The girl says, "I gotta quit now. I want to go in. I'm tired. I've got an early call. I've gotta get up. I've got lessons."

"Gees, let's not quit now honey. Oh no, not now!"
"Are you going to get out of the car and see me in?"
"No dear, I'm not."
"Why?"
"Because I can't move. Would you believe from here on down I'm cement?"
"You get out of the car. Be a gentleman."
"I'll try."
You get out of the car and the girl says a great line,
"You walk funny."
You neck for four hours gang and you'll walk funny! And you walk even funnier up the stairs.
"Wait on me Sally, wait on me."
One more kiss "mmmmmmmm." A little slow kiss, oh yeah. And then you crawl on your hands and knees down the steps, and you pick up a '38 Ford and throw it away.

Jonathan Winters
Jonathan Winters...Wings It!

You'll remember from the conditions of physical comedy that when you can guide the thoughts of the audience to high issues such as morality or ethics, then suddenly relate the same conversation to something physical, the surprising contrast causes laughter. Obscenity is an effective tool for this purpose.

Take, for instance, the ancient Greek play *Lysistrata*, where all the women of Athens refused to have sex with their husbands until the men end a horrible bloody war. At a crucial point, when the women's resistance is beginning to fray, the leading character, Lysistrata, speaks to her fellow townswomen. She extols the work they are doing, the social importance of their celibate cause, and the values they are reinforcing through their sacrifice. At the end of the speech, however she identifies with her comrades frustration by admitting, "We all want to get laid." The surprise of this admission at the end of such a long and moving speech causes laughter.

The role of comedians is to challenge society's rules, this role makes them a bit antisocial. Many people's favorite comedic characters in theatre, movies, and stand-up are the down-to-earth, foul-mouthed, tell-it-like-is slobs. The language of the comedians is the same we use, so we identify with them. And if they take verbal stabs at the high-and-mighty, we laugh at seeing the hero brought down to size. The language the comic uses cannot be too aggressive or vulgar, or we would see him as a too uncaring louse, we would not identify with him, and would lose our ability to laugh with him.

Comedians who became famous partly for their use of profanity are George Carlin, Richard Pryor, and Redd Fox. Fox had an in-your-face way of speaking, and made no bones about his language. A classic Fox line is, "I say shit and fuck for one reason—people *do*. I mean, if you ain't fucked, *shit*. If you ain't shit, *fuck!*" This is Redd's no nonsense way of saying that we are all too bashful about normal human activities and should lighten up a little.

Richard Pryor and George Carlin both used profanity, but they used it much different ways. Pryor's use of profanity was simply an extension of his environment; Carlin's was a calculated use of words to make a point. This is not to say that Carlin's humor was more intelligent or legitimate, not in the least. Both comedians were masters at their particular craft; however, Carlin's messages lay in the words themselves while Pryor used words to illuminate a different message.

Pryor commonly used profanity throughout his act, but it was actually part of his everyday speech. He used colloquialisms that were common to black Americans, words that were acceptable from one black to another, but not from whites to blacks. In fact, one of his earlier albums from 1976 was titled, "Bicentennial Nigger." African-Americans will often refer to each other using "nigger," an ironic use of a word that would inspire hate if used by other races, but one that promotes camaraderie when used by blacks themselves. Prior was born in 1941 in Peoria, Illinois and grew up in a brothel run by his grandmother, Marie Carter. His parents, Buck Carter and Gertrude Pryor, were working folks, a golden gloves boxer and a bookkeeper respectively. Neither parent had as much influence in raising Richard as his grandmother, who took him in after his mother left when he was ten. So Richard grew up on the streets of Peoria, with poolhalls, bars, and whorehouses as his playground. His education was the street, so his language and comic material were gleaned from it. Words like "nigger," "mothafucka," and "bitch," are sprinkled into his routines. This became Pryor's way of saying to his audiences, white and black, "I'm a black man, I will speak as I please and you better accept it."

Although many black entertainers of the time used these words in the company of their peers and for performing for black audiences, Pryor was the first to bring harsh street language to white audiences so unabashedly, especially for the tumultuous time of the '60s. In doing so he was able to bring black culture to all of America. This helped make his wonderful characters—an old drunk, a junkie, and a reverend, a barbecue shop owner, and the old codger, Mudbone—much more believable and enjoyable. Once he laid the groundwork with the audience, using his language to create a bond with them, his characters would enter using the same language. This truly based the characters in reality. Many comedians create characters that seem real. (Bob Newhart's trademark telephone conversations involve people we could easily imagine speaking to ourselves.) But Pryor's use of down-and-dirty foul language brought a harsh realism to his street-people characters.

He was one of the few comedians of his day who was not afraid of silence from the audience. Silence can strike fear into veteran and amateur comedians alike. Pryor would not alter his act simply because there wasn't a laugh every minute. His character routines were created not only to shock the audience with their audacity, but also to make pointed comments about the life black Americans face. One of his most popular characters was the black preacher who told it like it was:

We are gathered here today to celebrate this year of bicentenniality, in the hope of freedom and dignity. We are celebrating 200 years of...white folks kickin' ass. Now, white folks have had the essence of this understanding on their side for quite a while. However, we offer this prayer, and the prayer is, "How long...will this bullshit go on?" How long? How long? How long will this bullshit go on? That is the eternal question. Men have always asked, "How long?" When men first got here they asked, "How long...will these animals kick me in the ass? How long before I discover fire, and stop freezin' to death?" We always here, in the Church of Understanding and Unity, have tried to figure out how long? They say in the Bible we will know how long when a angel come up out of the sea. He will have seven heads, and a face like a serpent, and a body like a lion. I don't know about you, but I don't want to see no motherfucker who look like that! If I see him come up out of the water, I'm going to shoot him in the ass.

Richard Pryor
Bicentennial Nigger

Pryor got laughs in this routine not only for his directed comments about racial equality, but for having this kind of profanity come from the character of a reverend. We will talk more about the comedy of contrast in chapter seven, Character Contradiction. Pryor's courage in slapping the audience in the face with real-life characters and harsh dialogue paved the way for performers such as Whoopie Goldberg and Eric Bogosian.

At the time of this writing, Pryor was stricken with multiple sclerosis (MS), a degenerative disease that affects the victim's motor control by attacking the central nervous system. Although he is racked with pain and every simple movement or function is an ordeal, Pryor jokes about wanting to write a routine about MS. Of performing comedy about such a debilitating illness, Pryor says, "...that would be a mother."

George Carlin has become famous as a stand-up comedian primarily for his creative way of analyzing the English language. Lately he has begun to prove his acting talents in movies and television sit-coms, but no-one will forget his "Seven Words You Can Never Say on Television," and "The Difference Between Baseball and Football." As opposed to many comedians of today, who are merely taking advantage of looser than average censorship laws to shock the audience, Carlin never used foul language without ultimately making a point. The message could be soft and easy to digest, like the comparison of baseball to football. "...Football is more masculine than baseball. Just look at the terminology...in football you score a TOUCHDOWN, in baseball you *run home.*" Or the message could be a subtle comment on how we deal with others. "All any of us want is a place to put our stuff...but did you ever notice that somebody else's stuff is shit, and your shit is stuff? 'Hey, who moved my stuff and put their shit here? Who's shit is this by my stuff?'" Rather than a cheap way of getting laughs, Carlin's "Seven Words You Can't Say on Television" routine is a scathing commentary on censorship. He points out that the very words we use everyday can't even be used on a medium we watch everyday, even though some of the words actually sound pleasant.

"Tits" doesn't even belong on the list, you know. It's such a friendly sounding word. Sounds like a nickname, right? "Hey tits, come here man. Hey tits, meet toots. Toots, tits. Tits, toots." Sounds like a snack, doesn't it? Right! I don't mean your sexist snack. I mean new Nabisco Tits. Corn Tits, Pizza Tits, and Sesame Tits, and Onion Tits...Tator Tits. "Betcha can't eat just one!"

I'm not telling you what the other six words are. If you don't know the bit already, you'll have to buy a Carlin album. I'm not going to have angry mothers calling me because I put those filthy words in the book.

So, obscenity is an effective way to educate society as to its norms and expectations, as well as a light-hearted way to criticize those expectations. Just don't use it when your mother is listening.

Chapter 4
STORYLINE

"You'll never believe what she said then..."

Comedians of today have shifted away from the old joke-telling style of Henny Youngman and Bob Hope. Gone is the "Take my wife, please," or "Two guys walk into a bar" era of comedy. It has been replaced by the "This is my life, let me share it with you," comedian. Personal anecdotes and everyday observations make up the majority of today's comedy acts. In fact, if a comedian were to make joke-telling the majority of the act, the audience would tire of it quickly. This is because comedy audiences have matured and wised-up to the old tricks. In order to entertain these comedy-wise audiences comedians must stay ahead of the game and offer something new.

In the days of vaudeville a comedian was dealing with an audience that was not that familiar with live comedy. Back then a good show was a mixture of singing, dancing, striptease, and comedy, and the attention span of the listener was markedly shorter than the attentive nightclub crowds we are see today. Decades ago, material had to be repeated several times throughout the joke to ensure the audience heard and understood it:

So I says to the guy, "You should go see my friend Marty." He says, "I should see my friend Marty." He   *your friend Marty?" I says, "Yeah, says, "Why should I see your friend*

Marty?" And I says, "You want to know why you should see my friend Marty?" And he says, "Yeah, I want to know."(Joke goes on ad infinitum.)

In the short passage above a single thought is repeated three or four times. The same joke told today would fail miserably with the audience saying, "Get to the point already!" This is not merely a difference in style. Comedy *reflects* the tastes of the day much more than it *dictates* them. Since comedians work for a laugh in the most efficient way possible, they will respond to the sensibilities of the audience, creating material that will suit the needs of the listener.

As comedy has matured, audiences have increased their expectations of comedians. Years ago, a goofy character was enough to inspire laughter. Now a performer needs to convey a sense of reality in his or her act. Even goofy characters of today have changed. Lovable buffoons of old comedy (Lou Costello, Jack Benny's sidekick Rochester, and Jerry Lewis) have largely been replaced by comedians who are just as odd (Bobcat Goldthwait, Emo Phillips, Carrot Top), but have solid material to back up the foolishness (Jim Carey and Pee Wee Herman notwithstanding).

An audience wants to believe what they are hearing, making it easier to become immersed in the material. One-liner jokes give the audience the sense that the comedian is *trying* to make them laugh. An interesting paradox exists in comedy, although an audience goes to a comedy club or play for the express purpose of laughing, if they feel the comedian is trying to make them laugh they will actively fight against it. Laughter allows us to exert power and control, if someone looks like they are trying to make us laugh they are trying to exert control over us, which takes us in the opposite direction of laughter.

One-liner jokes inherently include the goal of laughter, and this quality causes the audience to lose the sense of realism in the joke that is necessary for them to laugh. Stories are a perfect replacement. A theatrical production, by its nature, avoids the problem of "pushing for a laugh," since the characters in the story already seem to be *living the plot*. Comedians now are taking advantage of this style by weaving stories into comedy acts. Stories contain an innate sense of reality that helps produce laughter.

Many comedians simply embellish true stories from their life to create humor, making it easier for them to commit to the story's delivery. There are two advantages to this type of humor. First, the audience believes the comedian actually experienced the story, no matter how outlandish the circumstances; second, there is no point in the story where it is obvious that the audience is *supposed* to laugh. This removes some risk for the comedian, the risk of failure. If a comedian tells a joke it is obvious to the audience when they are supposed to laugh. If that point comes and the audience doesn't find it funny, they realize that the comedian has failed. Failure on the comedians part makes the audience nervous, which is a terrible deterrent to laughter. If told well, a story does not appear to have one point at which the audience is supposed to laugh, so if they do it's a bonus; if they don't, nothing is lost.

Storyline is the first level of comedy to emphasize the importance of the comedian's attitude of delivery. Profanity carries its own attitude so much less is required of the comedian. Since the elements of a story may simply be an embellishment of the truth, the humor often must come from the way the story is told, not the actual wording. A strong attitude on the part of the comedian provides a sense of reality, helping us believe that the experience was actually lived. The use of plot requires the teller to include many smaller punchlines throughout the story to maintain interest and help build up to a climactic conclusion. So, the humor of storyline is challenging because it requires the teller to inject many laugh points while still keeping the story believable.

The humor of storyline includes many elements— misunderstandings among the characters in the plot, mistaken identities, cross purposes, and secret plans. A great influence on modern storyline was the French playwright Georges Faydeau (1862-1921). Faydeau is known as the creator of the "Faydeau Farce." A Faydeau Farce involved a story that revolved around two main characters. If these two characters ever met face-to-face in the play, catastrophe would strike, usually because either the main characters or other characters in the play had secret schemes that would be exposed as a result. Throughout the entire play the two characters would repeatedly come to within a hair's breadth of each other, but something would always happen at the last minute to keep them from discovering each other. AS one would walk in one door, the other would be just leaving through another. While speaking to one main character, a minor character would almost let slip the secret and have to do a quick verbal tap-dance to cover the scheme. Or one character would suggest visiting a restaurant, which would result in discovering the other character, and wacky servants would have to quickly devise plans to separate the two.

The audience is brought to the edge of their seats over and over, until the anticipation of the inevitable meeting is almost too much to bear. At the climax, the two characters finally meet and everything turns out for the best; the evil characters are punished, the good ones are rewarded, and the hero and heroine fall in love and get married. The most enjoyable part of the play for the audience is witnessing the disaster just about to happen—a door swinging open and a character entering unexpectedly, or two enemies unknowingly cross the stage with their backs to each other. Sometimes the situation was reversed, and the meeting of the two characters would result in something good. So the audience begins to root for the two to get together, but are disappointed throughout the play as circumstances keep popping up to prevent it.

Faydeau was a master at creating fast-paced and intricate plots. He also developed the technique of multiple doors. In his play "Hotel Paradiso," characters ran in and out of rooms so fast, with doors opening and closing with such clockwork timing, that the actors always seemed on the verge of running into each other and discovering the "wrong" person. The speed and intricacy of the play is a wonder to watch and has influenced the design of comedy sets even today. This style and use of doors was also used by Michael Frayn in London, in 1982 in his very popular play, *Noises Off*, which later had successful runs in America and became a movie with the same name. I strongly recommend experiencing this wonderful style of comedy, it will give you a good idea where most of today's comedy styles originated.

Television has not lost the love of a good farce. Almost every sit-com has, at one point or another, used the classic Faydeau Farce formula. From Ralph Kramden, in "The Honeymooners," trying to hide his gambling winnings from his wife, to Bill Cosby running through his house looking for his children who happen to be following right behind him. Many modern comedy stars owe their inspiration to the old masters. Some sit-coms revolved entirely around the hidden-identity theme. "Three's Company," "Bosom Buddies," "I Dream of Jeannie," "My Mother the Car," " Mr. Ed," "My Favorite Martian," and "Bewitched" all had plots that rested on the notion that one main character had a secret identity that was shared by only one or two other characters. In all these television shows, if an "outsider" were to discover the secret identity there would be big trouble (and wacky hijinks). If a sit-com has not used hidden identities and secret plans as its main focus, it has surely used them for a number of episodes or sub-plots. The character of Greg Brady in "The Brady Bunch," dressed up in a manly disguise to impress a girlfriend and to avoid being discovered by his parents. Barney Fife, of "The Andy Griffith Show," dressed up like an old cleaning lady to try to catch the bank guard snoozing on the job. Next time you flick on the TV see how the techniques of a classic playwright like Feydeau continue to influence modern television writers. The irony is, many television writers have never heard of Faydeau. They grew up watching TV and use older shows for inspiration, in effect, copying those who copied those who copied Faydeau.

Although plot or storyline humor gets its laughter from many sources, the main source is *the audience is aware of something the characters in the story are not.* Imagine a common plot in a sit-com, a boy comes home with a bad report card and wants to hide it from his parents so he won't get in trouble and be grounded from the school dance that night. He hides the report card in his pillow. Later we see his father gathering up linen to do the laundry. We see the father discover the report card. Later at the dance we see the boy boasting to his friends about fooling his parents. We then see the father show up at the dance as a surprise chaperone. The father doesn't reveal his knowledge of the report card immediately, he wants to set his son up for a confession. The boy knows something is amiss, but can't quite figure out what. The rest of the night is a game of dodge between the father and son as the boy tries to see what the father is up to, and the father playing the boy like a fish on a line. A small amount of laughter occurs first when the father discovers the report card in the pillowcase. The moment we saw the father discover the report card we were "in on the joke." This is precisely where everyone loves to be, on the side of the joke *giver*, not the joke *getter*. To deliver the joke is to be in control; to be the butt of the joke is to made the fool. We now know that the father is going to "get" the boy, and we have fun trying to figure out how. The second laugh comes as the boy is bragging to his friends and the father walks in. Our attitude is, "O.K. Mr. Sure-of-Yourself, what are you going to do now?" The closer the father gets to revealing the boy's lie the more humor we experience. We are aware of something the boy is not and our own sense of power is heightened to delight.

The hit stage and movie production, *Fiddler on the Roof* has a great scene that involves the storyline convention of informing the audience of a fact of which the characters are unaware. Yente, the village matchmaker, has come to the home of Tevye, a poor dairyman, and his wife Golde. Tevye is not home so the two women sit down to discuss Yente's surprise news. It seems she has found what she considers to be a perfect husband for Tevye and Golde's eldest daughter, Tzeitel. The village butcher, Lazar Wolf, has taken a liking to her. The time and place of the story is old Russia, and Jewish customs of the time dictate that the father must agree to the match, so Lazar Wolf can pay the matchmaker her fee and he and Tzeitel can marry. (The whole process is decided without consulting the daughter. After all, she's only a child. What could she know of these things?) Golde is ecstatic at the possibility of finding a husband for Tzeitel, especially since they are a poor family and can not afford the traditional dowry to offer a prospective husband. As well, they have five daughters all together, and finding a husband for one lessens their burden. Golde tells Yente that she loves her choice of a man, but is afraid Tevye will not agree, since Lazar is a butcher and Tevye wants his daughters to marry scholars and learned men. Yente tells Golde not to worry. "Listen Golde," she says, "You send Tevye to him. Don't tell him what it's about. Let Lazar discuss it himself. He'll win him over. He's a good man and a wealthy man."

Already we as audience see that this will lead to trouble. We have learned from our own lives that anytime information is kept from someone it will lead to mistaken intentions and disaster. Later, when Golde tells Tevye that Lazar wants to see him, and that all she knows is that it is concerning an important matter, Tevye assumes incorrectly. "If he's thinking about buying my new milk cow, he can forget it," Tevye bellows. Heeding Yente's advise, Golde does not correct him, lest she reveal that she knows the nature of the meeting. Besides, she knows that Tevye doesn't really care for Lazar, and she wouldn't want to look eager to defend him. The stage is set for us viewers. We know what the meeting is about, we know that Tevye mistakenly thinks Lazar wants his cow, and we know that Lazar sent the matchmaker to Tevye's house so he assumes Tevye knows about his desire for a wife. We know a mix-up is on the way, and the meeting doesn't disappoint us:

Lazar: Tevye...
Tevye: Yes?
Lazar: I suppose you know why I wanted to see you.
Tevye: Oh yes, I do, but there is no use talking about it.

Lazar: (a bit taken aback by the sudden opposition) Ahhh...Tevye, I understand how you feel, but...ahhh...after all, you have a few more without her.

Tevye: Ahhh, I see. Today you want one, tomorrow you may want two.

Lazar: Two! Wha...What would I do with two?

Tevye: The same as you do with one.

Lazar: (very confused, begins to think that Tevye is toying with him) Tevye...this is...very important to me.

Tevye: Why is it so important to you?

Lazar: Frankly...because...I'm lonely.

Tevye: Lonely? Lazar, what are you talking about? How can a little cow keep you company?

Lazar: Little cow! Is that what you call her?

Tevye: What else should I call her? That's what she is! Lazar, what are you talking about?

Lazar: Don't you know?

Tevye: Of course I know! We are talking about my new milk cow, the one you want to buy from me.

At this point the cross meaning is revealed and the humor reaches its climax. It is a classic example of misunderstanding and illustrates the prime source of storyline laughter, *we know something they don't.*

It is important to distinguish between the comedy of the story, and the comedy of the characters within the story. If two people run around the house looking for each other, and then begin flailing at each other wildly when they finally meet, two forms of humor exist. The chase involves storyline, the fight involves physical comedy. Part of our laughter in the *Fiddler on the Roof* scene does involve the characters themselves, how absurdly they behave and how exaggerated their reactions are to each other. Most of the humor of the scene however is derived from the situation that Tevye and Lazar have thrust upon them. As in all good storyline humor, the characters have no control over the events that affect them.

A good storyline actually takes on a life of its own to create humor. The story appears to be a creature that is acting on the characters, controlling them. The characters seem unable to change their own destiny. Like robots they go through the motions dictated to them. Like Henri Bergson's "Jack-in-the-box" theory, the characters repeat the same motions over and over again, to no avail. They are victims of circumstance.

The human-like characteristic of the plot adds to the comic potential. It is almost as if a young child were playing with the characters. Or, as many have said, God is using us for his own amusement by creating these impossible situations.

Chapter 5
LANGUAGE

Stuffy Woman: *Hold me closer...closer...closer.*
Groucho Marx: *If I held you any closer, I'd be behind you.*

Language is the point at which the gap between high and low comedy is the greatest. All of the areas of comedy up to this point on the pyramid can be enjoyed with relatively little intellect. Babies and toddlers enjoy physical comedy, young children get a kick out of obscenity, and children as young as five or six can follow a simple storyline. To appreciate the comedy of language, however, one must command an extensive vocabulary and understand the meaning and intent of dialogue. As Freud said, *"Wit is made, the comical is found."* In this sense, physical comedy is discovered, obscenity is enforced, storyline leads the viewer, but language is a product of higher cognitive thought. In order for the humor of language to work, the audience must make the association between what is actually said and what is implied or expressed conceptually. This puts a greater burden on the listener and on the comedian, who must make sure that the humor can still be understood and appreciated by all audience members. Humor of language can be divided into four areas: sarcasm, repartee, irony, and absurdity.

Which category the humor falls into depends on whether it is meant to ridicule or be ridiculous.

Sarcasm

Sarcasm, the aggressive insult of a person or institution, is an interesting characteristic in humans and may actually be a result of evolution. Some theorists believe that laughter evolved from as far back as when humans were apes. When two apes meet, they immediately see who is the stronger to determine their hierarchy in the tribe. After the battle, while the loser lays on the ground in submission, the victor will throw his head back and let out a victory cry. Since physical battle is no longer an acceptable means of settling a dispute, we battle with words, and the victory cry is laughter.

Roz: "Wait a minute. Are you saying that blind dates are okay for your father, but not for you?"

Frasier: "Yes, that also goes for games with balls, domestic beer, and giant   trucks that roll over smaller ones."

"Frasier"
NBC/Paramount

We all have a need to position ourselves in society, especially with those close to us. This "tribe" determines our sense of self-worth. Many still rely on physical strength to show dominance, as evidenced by the number of people pumping iron every day in gyms across the country. (I personally never understood lifting weights, I figure if I can't lift something, I'll get someone to help me.) Anyway, we certainly can't go around beating each other up every time we have a dispute (our mothers would frown on that), and we can't have arm-wrestling contests to see who is going to mate with whom. Sarcasm has taken over as the evolved human's way of establishing superiority. In today's society, the smarter person will undoubtedly gain the most wealth and status, so more weight is placed on quick wit and brains than on muscle.

The effective use of language and sarcastic humor were necessary skills for writers in the days of radio. Without the benefit of visual humor, radio writers had to create dialogue that would hook the listener for the entire show. Good character development was as important then as it is in today's serial programs (if you can call what you see on a soap opera "character development"). Don Ameche and Francis Langford played two wonderful characters in the radio program, "The Bickersons." Each episode of the program followed the same premise: John Bickerson works two or three jobs at a time to try to satisfy his wife, Blanche, in her quest for a better life. Blanche is never satisfied, always wanting a larger apartment, a new TV, or a new house. She nags at him constantly, never letting him do the one thing he so desperately wants in every episode—sleep. Here are excerpts from various programs:

John: (just coming home, tired from a new job) *Ooo am I beat.*

Blanche: (cheerfully) *John, is that you?*
Yes it's me.

How's the new job dear?

I hate it.

You hate it?

Yes, I hate it. And I'm glad I hate it, because if I didn't hate it I'd like it and I hate it. Is the kettle on the stove?

No, I didn't know what time you were coming home. Are you going off to bed?

No. I'm going to make some hot tea and bathe my feet.

Can't you bathe your feet in plain water?

I am going to bathe them in plain water. I want some hot tea to drink. You go to sleep.

(Blanche is now upset as well) *Well I don't see any reason for you to be so   disagreeable, John. I haven't done anything to you.*

(Sarcastically) *No, you haven't done anything. All day and all night you beef about getting a bigger place to live in. It isn't bad enough I work like a   slave on one job, you force me to take another one. I'm so tired I can't   see.*

I don't see why we should live in this rat's nest when all our friends have such lovely homes. You can't blame me for wanting to better myself.

Well stop wanting to better me.

It's a wife's duty to see that her husband gets ahead in this world. You can't say I'm not trying, John.

No Blanche, I can't say you're not trying. You're the most trying woman I ever   met in my life.

In another episode, John is asleep snoring so loud that Blanche can't sleep.

(Loud snores that get more outlandish with each one)
Blanche: (to herself) He's been like that for three hours. (to John) John, turn over on your side. Go on.
(Snore)
B: Wake up, wake up.
John: (very drowsy) *Wake up, what's wrong? What's the matter Blanche?*
You've got to stop it John. I can't lie here another minute and listen to those awful noises.
Awful.
Why must I suffer all my life? You can stop that snoring if you want to, I know you can. No other man snores like you.
How do you know?
I talk to my women friends. Their husbands are so quiet they have to keep waking them to see if they're dead. What I wouldn't give to be able to sleep through the night just once.
Me too.
And not to hear that snarling, and rasping, and whining, and roaring. Honest John, who else carries on like that?
Honest John.
Very funny. Oh you're so funny John Bickerson.
No I'm not funny Blanche, I'm just sleepy.
Well what about me? I haven't slept for so long I'm a nervous wreck. My face is full of lines. I've changed into a withered old crow.

You haven't changed since the day I married you. (pause)
You look great.
  That's not true. You're just trying to make me feel good.
  I am not.
  You are too.
  I am not! I wouldn't make you feel good if it was the last
thing I ever did!

Sarcasm as a means of social positioning explains the use of jokes against certain members of society. Jokes about ethnic groups, women, and gays have had their popularity rise and fall over the decades. When a society of animals form, there is usually a pecking order established, and once that order is fixed, any outsider is tested until they establish themselves in the group. American humor has a tradition of mocking foreign dialects, religions, and cultures. As groups of people assimilate into our society, they are the target of sarcastic humor until we understand them well enough that they no longer seem strange to us. If humans ever evolved to the point where they didn't care about their status in a group, their use of sarcasm would most likely disappear. I wouldn't hold your breath.

Ever since Jack Parr first hosted *The Tonight Show*, the opening monologue has been famous for scathing reviews of the days events. Sarcasm is a very effective tool for equalizing people, which is why it is often directed at leaders of society. Ever since George Washington's aide called him "Ol' Wooden Mouth" behind his back, presidents have been the target of jokes. Not only are these jokes a way to voice our dissatisfaction of their actions, but a way to bring these larger-than-life figures down to size. It is a simple way of confronting the apes that rule the tribe without meeting them face-to-face.

Perhaps the most famous purveyor of sarcastic venom is Don Rickles. He made a career out of stabbing anyone who was near enough, and unlucky enough, to catch his eye. The interesting thing about Rickles, however, is that he was really the first to venture into the risky territory of sarcasm against the helpless. Comedy is known for attacking those in positions of power. Giving the comedian the quickest and surest way to make an ally of the audience. Rickles wasn't satisfied with the easy target, and frequently picked on old ladies, children, the clergy—in fact anyone sitting in the audience would find themselves the victim of Rickles, most often for no reason at all. *"Nice dress lady, we'll take up a collection for you after the show."* Where most comedians of the day waited for an audience member to heckle them, thereby exposing themselves as a willing target, Rickles went looking for game, big and small, and opened up the genre to a stream of followers. Since Rickles pioneered the skewering style of sarcasm, other comedians have followed in his footsteps....

"I like this gentleman here in the audience. He's the kind of guy who gets dressed in the morning and says, "If it doesn't say John Deere on it, I'm not wearing it. And this lady over here. A prime example that if you drink, please do not do your own hair."

Michael Dane, Comedian

Repartee

Repartee is the same as sarcasm in that it is meant to demean another, except that it involves a back-and-forth verbal contest between two people. The audience delights in seeing an open battle of wits. Sometimes the battle is entirely on stage, sometimes between performer and audience member. On-stage repartee is a style made popular by duo acts such as Dean Martin and Jerry Lewis, Sonny and Cher, the Smothers Brothers, Dan Rowan and Dick Martin of the television show, "Laugh-In", and Abbott and Costello. Even today, hosts of "The Tonight Show," and "Late Night" will banter back and forth with their orchestra leaders and guests for the main source of comedy in the show. Many comedians today prefer to let the audience be their partner. One can always count on at least one loudmouth in every crowd, and they are rarely equipped to do battle with a professional comedian. In the most effective repartee, the true intent of the speaker is veiled. If, in insult, we say the blunt vernacular, *"You look butt-ugly,"* in repartee we hide the insult, *"That's a lovely sweater, I think it's great that some people still wear those old styles."*

Comedy duos rely heavily on the humor of repartee, which is both a blessing and a challenge for them. As with all humor of language, timing and delivery are vital. Writing for two people provides the opportunity to build the set-up lines into the script. There's no need to wait for an audience member to jump in, the performers can be more sure of their pacing. Repartee is a challenge to write because the dialogue must seem natural and believable. To this end, good comedy duos establish strong characters and let the dialogue reflect that character. In this way, the lines seem believable and also become easier to write as the character becomes more and more defined. With Abbott & Costello you always knew Bud Abbott was the sly smooth talker and Lou Costello was the rube who was either going to get taken or would screw up Bud's plans. Many of Abbott & Costello's routines centered around the misunderstanding of words, as in the following:

Costello, take that horse outside right now and turn him loose.

Wait a minute, Abbott. I can't do that. Peanut Butter is hungry and I gotta feed   him. Hey, what does a horse eat?

A horse? Well, a horse eats his fodder.

He eats his fodder?

Certainly.

That's fine. And what does the horses fodder eat?

He eats his fodder.

*Well what do you know? And what does a horse's **mudder** eat?*

She eats her fodder.

*What are they, **cannibals**?*

Certainly not. Every horse has to eat his fodder.

Oh I see. He eats his fodder...

Yes

... and then his fodder eats his fodder...

That's it.

...and then his mudder eats her fodder. And the next thing you know, there won't be no fodders left for Fodder's Day.

They move on to discuss the upcoming race

...Costello that broken down horse doesn't belong on a racetrack. Who'd ever bet on a nag like that?

I would.

You would?

I'm gonna take all my money outa my piggy bank. I'm even gonna sell my Erector Set and my ping pong paddles...

You're going to sell all that? For what?

I'm going to put every cent of my money on my horse.

No, that's ridiculous Costello. Putting all your money on a horse. Big gamblers don't do that.

Oh no? Well the biggest gambler that ever lived did it.

And just who was the biggest gambler that ever lived?

Lady Godiva.

Lady Godiva was a gambler?

Yup! She put everything she had on a horse.

In repartee we see a clear example of the "two apes battling in the woods" theory. As opposed to other forms of comedy, in repartee we delight in actually seeing the fight taking place. Repartee satisfies the comedian's desire to engage in verbal confrontation, and the audiences desire to see a beating. Take the daily battle between the characters, Murray Slaughter and

Tedd Baxter (played by Ted Knight, and Gavin MacLeod), from The Mary Tyler Moore Show. The on-going slinging of insults between the two defined their entire relationship.

Tedd: *I hope [the new boss] is not mad at me. I'd hate to get fired for a little pinch-a-rini in the elevator."*
Murray: *Tedd, if you go, I go.*
Tedd: *Do you mean that, Murray?*
Murray: *Absolutely, I couldn't write for anyone else.*
Ted: *Really?*
Murray: *Really. My vocabulary isn't what it used to be.*

Those who engage in repartee not only want to dominate the opponent, but those in attendance as well. This is demonstrated when a group of friends gather and start trading insults and put-downs. There always appears to be one person who has to have the last word, establishing dominance over the group. A modern form of this contest is called "the dozens," played primarily by inner-city youth. The object is to see who can create the most extravagant insult, usually about someone's mother. *"Your mother is so stupid, she let the baby walk around for two weeks without changing his diapers because the box said they were good for up to 24 pounds." "Yeah? Well your momma's so fat she goes to the movies and sits next to everybody."*

Repartee is a very popular tool of television comedy.

Diane: *"Carla, I have to step out. Could you cover my tables for me for a   while."*

Carla: *"Sure. I'll act geeky, won't serve 'em for 20 minutes, and I'll bring all the   wrong drinks. They'll never know you were gone."*

"Cheers"
NBC/Paramount Productions

Much of our laughter in any situation is caused by a release of tension.   Comic situations create a build-up of tension. Wondering about the outcome of a situation or guessing what the surprise will be is like knowing that a bomb is definitely going to explode, but not knowing just when. The climax of the situation allows for a release of tension through laughter. This same condition applies to verbal repartee. The "fight" between the two speakers creates a build-up of tension, and the winner, the speaker getting the last word, ends the conflict. The resulting release of tension is manifested in laughter. Perhaps the prehistoric man who won the physical battle was simply releasing tension when he let out a victory cry.

Sometimes humorous repartee can be achieved even if the participants show no aggression or sarcastic intent. The TV actress Lisa Kudrow, best known as the ditsy character Phoebe on "Friends," also played a waitress on the sit-com "Mad About You." Both the waitress character and Phoebe are similar in that they have no idea that what they say is funny.

Kudrow (as the waitress): *Will you have the usual today, sir?*

Customer: *Why yes, I will.*

Kudrow: *And what is that?*

"Mad About You"

NBC/Paramount Productions

What makes Kudrow's character funny is that she is responding with a wonderful come-back, and is not even aware of it. If the line were delivered by another, more savvy character, we would suspect that the line, "Will you have the usual today, sir?" was a set-up to draw the customer in and insult him by not knowing his usual order, thereby declaring his insignificance. Kudrow's character is a wonderful re-creation of the style of George Burns' comedy partner, Gracie Allen. Allen's character walked the line between being a complete airhead and really knowing more than she let on. Her misunderstandings of peoples words were her trademark.

Photographer: *How about a picture with you and Mr. Burns?*

Allen: *All right.* (Burns and Allen stand arm in arm)

Photographer: *How about a hug?*

Allen: *All right.* (she takes the camera from him, hands it to George, and hugs the photographer)

Irony

Isn't it ironic that most people know what irony is, but they can't really define it? Irony involves a twist in language, some

69

kind of paradox or contradiction. Many people confuse irony with coincidence. *"Isn't it ironic that you and I both came to the same grocery store at the same time."* That is, in fact coincidence. It would be *ironic* if you both came to the same grocery store to buy the other person something they needed so they wouldn't have to go to the grocery store.

Edgar Johnson describes irony in <u>A Treasury of Satire</u> as "overstating what we don't mean and carefully understating what we do mean... saying more and more of what we don't mean until, at last, the intensification of understatement results in inversion." Irony differs from sarcasm and repartee in that it is a *non-aggressive* form of humor. In irony, implied meaning can be hidden well enough that the listener is allowed to make connections that are actually a reverse of what is said (an inversion).

Jethro: *Are you going to leave the tonic here in the hospital for Mrs. Drysdale, Granny?*

Granny: *No! It takes a highly qualified doctor to dispense this tonic. And you're not likely to find one of them in a hospital!*

"The Beverly Hillbillies"

By hiding what we mean in convoluted statements we are building up confusion and tension in the mind of the listener. If this were to occur in a non-comedic setting, such as a lecture, our frustration would grow and grow throughout the lecture for as long as we were unable to understand the speaker. I regularly

70

used this excuse for sleeping during classes at college, it never worked. Many students, when faced with a particularly confusing professor, simply give up taking notes and hope someone else knows what is going on so they can copy homework later. That never worked for me either.

People want to understand what is said to them. The brain works at such a high speed that if we have to slow down our normal rate of thinking to reconsider something, it is frustrating. So confusion causes tension. Consider the last time a friend asked you a question and you didn't hear it clearly. You asked him to repeat the question. He asked the question again, and again you didn't understand. Then you asked him again to repeat it, only this time you asked louder and more forcefully. By the fifth round of question and confusion you just gave up and said, "Yeah, sure thing." I discovered personally that this is a good way to unknowingly loan your car to someone for a month.

In a comedic setting, the build-up of tension due to confusion is released when the misunderstanding is cleared up. The body relaxes, the listener breathes a sigh of relief saying, "Oh, *now* I get it." Observe the next time you see someone trying to understand a foreign guest with a heavy dialect. The confusion is great fun (as long as you're the one watching).

> Foreign guest: *Do-ah gi da bahs dah-laiva a wa dahla bi?*
> Friend: *Pardon me?*
> Foreign guest: *Do-ah **gi** da bahs **dah-laiva** a wa dahla bi?*
> Friend: *I'm sorry. Again.*
> Foreign guest: *Do-ah **gi** da **bahs dah**-laiva a **wa** dahla **bi?**

71

When the two finally realize that the guest is trying to say, "Do I the bus driver a one dollar bill?" they let out a laugh. The laugh is both a release and a show of delight that the object of confusion was such a simple phrase.

Irony creates small reactions to the build-up of tension that occurs in normal conversation. The release is small because the misunderstanding is made clear by using familiar and expected terms and descriptions. When misunderstanding is part of a comedy routine, the build-up of tension is usually greater because the comedian wishes to create a bigger pay-off and must stretch out the misunderstanding. To do this, dissimilar subjects are paired in conversation, complicated language is used, and the real meaning is kept hidden from the listener for as long as possible.

A good comedian builds up just as much incongruity as needed to lead to the audience away from the surprise ending without confusing them so much that they won't understand the conclusion. If the real meaning of what is being said involves an incongruous contrast and the environment is lighthearted, the release of tension is accompanied by laughter. If the environment were not lighthearted, at a lecture for example, the release of tension would not be accompanied by laughter and would probably just be a surprised look and a relaxing of the body.

An ironic situation involves giving emphasis to a situation by stating its opposite. This is part of what gives irony its humor. When our brain realizes the correlation between two opposites, we laugh. See how stating the opposite provides emphasis in the following news reports from United Press International (UPI):

An Indianapolis man, (name withheld) cited by police in June in a traffic collision that killed a woman in another car, said he ran the red light because he was thinking too intensely about material he had learned the day before in a defensive-driving course.

In May, (a woman) who is in a halfway house in Tampa, FL, the result of a 1990 trial in which she was found not guilty by reason of insanity for strangling her two toddlers, petitioned to be released because she has a job lined up. According to a counselor, a local couple wants to hire her as a baby sitter.

There is no question that the above reports are ironic. Whether or not you laugh at them depends on your sensibilities. If you are too sensitive to the events in the story, you may be too dismayed to laugh. If the ironic twist is powerful enough you may laugh in spite of your personal feelings about the subject. As will be discussed in the chapter, "The Perfect Setting," we must be detached from the people in the story or event. If we feel too much for the characters we are too concerned to laugh.

A less weighty and more common form of irony is the pun, which relies not on a play on words or situations, but a play on the sounds of words. Many people hate puns. When the speaker in a comedic situation is leading up to a climax we begin to anticipate a clever conclusion. An audience likes to work a little for a laugh. We derive great satisfaction from successfully connecting intricate meanings and figuring out twists in language. If we are set-up to believe that a big pay-off is coming and the result is simply a pun, our expectations have not been met. It's the same as if your parents built up your expectations for a birthday present for weeks before the party and when the day arrived they gave you a pen and pencil set. Besides being the mental equivalent of giving a starving dog a rubber bone, a pun is unsatisfying to most people because they are aware that they are capable of creating puns themselves, so the creator displays no special talent. Puns rarely achieve full throated laughs. Most people who use them only get the satisfaction of having "tricked" the listener into thinking something more was coming. That is another reason laughter is stifled. As I mentioned earlier, people do not like to be controlled. Laughter must come as a delightful surprise. When the joke-teller displays that he or she is trying to create a laugh we will fight against laughing. A pun is a most obvious attempt at laughter, and creates little of it.

A more complicated form of pun is the *double entendre*, or "double meaning." It involves more than just the similarity in sounds of words, it mixes meanings in clever ways.

"Your honor, the prostitution rests."
Bob Novisky, playing an attorney in
The Stevie Ray's Comedy Troupe

The above statement not only utilizes the pun, with "prosecution" and "prostitution" sounding the same, but also uses the meaning of the words to make a statement. The statement of the prostitute laying down, or resting, creates images in our mind that are in contrast to the atmosphere of a courtroom. We know what the attorney intended to say, which allows us to do some of the mental work to create the joke. Irony is satisfying because of its ability to veil important statements. When we discover the true meaning behind what is said we appreciate the attitude of the speaker. So, laughter at ironic statements may involve a feeling of "take *that*" from the listener.

Groucho Marx: *Oh, hello Pierre. I see you've been out for a walk with your girl.*

Pierre: *Yes we have.*

Groucho: *So when are you two lovebirds getting married?*

Pierre: *Oh, marriage is impossible*

Groucho: *Not until after you're married.*

Most people would laugh at what Groucho said, because of its twist on the use of language and how Groucho sets up the unsuspecting Pierre. Those who have had any trouble in a relationship would laugh because of Groucho's stab at marriage. The statement is a veiled insult of marriage because Groucho's attitude at first appears that he wants the two love birds to get married, he then surprises us with his true opinion. He also allows us to do some of the quick mental work by not stating his opinion straight out. If he had said, "I think marriage is bad," we would have simply heard an opinion. It would sound like

Groucho was preaching or lecturing to us. Neither of these conditions incite laughter. Instead he says an incomplete sentence. He makes us connect his statement with the one uttered just before to determine his meaning. Our connecting of the two statements to create meaning is the mental work we love to do to create our own laugh. This approach allows the speaker and the audience to work together. It is this cooperation that creates the atmosphere conducive to laughter. In this way, the same sentiment that would cause debate or argument if expressed in a simple conversation, instead causes laughter.

Absurdity

Absurdity is also a non-aggressive form of language humor. In contrast to the previous three forms, absurdity involves the use of nonsensical language, or language that contorts meaning, such as "It was so dark you couldn't see your face in front of you." Whereas irony contains hidden meanings or feelings of the speaker, absurdity can carry a hidden meaning seemingly unknown to the speaker. Take for instance TV's Archie Bunker who said, *"I ain't going to no Catholic church with some priest talking all that mumbo jumbo and sprinkling incest all over everybody."* On the surface this seems like a simple mix-up on Archie's part, but given the tenets of the church against deviant sexuality it also makes a strong social comment. What makes it funny, besides it's absurdity, is that Archie is completely unaware of the true meaning of his statement. If Archie were more adept at language and said, "I hate the Catholic church. They're a bunch of hypocrites!" We would see him as opinionated, but not particularly funny. And if he showed us that he was *aware* he was being funny by emphasizing what he knew was funny about his statement (i.e. *"I ain't going to no Catholic church with some priest talking all that mumbo jumbo and sprinkling incest all over everybody."*) we would not be allowed to create the laugh ourselves. His spoon-feeding us the laugh would kill it for us. We may laugh in agreement with his opinion of the Catholic church, but the laughter would be from sarcasm, not absurdity.

The type of absurd language Archie used above is often called a "malapropism." It got its name from the character, Mrs. Malaprop, in Richard Brinsley Sheridan's 1775 play, *The Rivals*. Sheridan developed a comic character in Malaprop by having her constantly mix meanings and phrases so the other characters in the play had to think twice about everything she said. Consider the following statements made by Mrs. Malaprop in *The Rivals*.

"But the point we would request of you is, that you will promise to forget this fellow—to illiterate him, I say, from your memory"

"Observe me, Sir Anthony—I would by no means wish a daughter of mine to be a progeny of learning...I would send her, at nine years old, to a boarding school in order to learn a little ingenuity and artifice...and, as she grew up, I would have her instructed in geometry, that she might know something of the contagious countries...."

Many modern comedians mirror the comedy techniques of playwrights and comedians of centuries ago. The language of Mrs. Malaprop of 1775 is almost exactly the same as that of one of America's most famous comedians, Norm Crosby. This is not to say that Mr. Crosby borrowed from *The Rivals* for his act, but it does illustrate that comedy ideas seem to follow a cycle. What makes this type of mix-up funny is not only the fact that the comedian is completely unaware of his mistake, but also that he is somewhat arrogant about his opinion. Mrs. Malaprop is very forceful about what kind of education her daughter should receive, and yet shows a lack of education in her mistaken use of the word, *contagious*.

Human nature is such that we love to see people who are in power brought down to our level. We scrutinize people who act self-important, any little slip of the tongue is ammunition for ridicule. Remember the last time your boss was giving a presentation and stumbled over his words? You may not have laughed at the time, but you sure shared a chuckle about it with your co-workers in the break room.

Mrs. Malaprop and Archie Bunker are both absolutely sure of how the world should be. Mrs. Malaprop makes an absurd and ironic statement by saying that she would not want her daughter to engage in higher learning, only to follow the statement with a comment that displays her own ignorance. Archie openly attacks other races and religions, only to show by his language that he has no clear understanding of them.

Children delight in absurd language because of its playful nature. Dr. Suess used this quality in his books with such expertise that his writings have been the favorite of children for generations. He used absurdity not only to please the child, but to put children and adults on an even playing field in the world of his story. Instead of children having to ask, "What does that word mean?" as they would with any other book, the child and adult would both be assaulted with page after page of silly fictitious words like "wuzzle" and "thneed." The child would know that these words are meant only for fun, and they could enjoy the book even more. Suess attacked the English language wonderfully in his book, On Beyond Zebra, in which he claims that there are actually more than twenty six letters in the alphabet. Each letter is defined in terms of the object or animal to which it relates. For example, the letter "fuddle" is used to spell the name of a bird, "Miss Fuddle-dee-Duddle," and "glikk" is used in the name of a juggling insect, the "glikker."

So, on beyond Zebra!
Explore!
Like Columbus!
Discover New Letters!
Like WUM is for Wumbus,
My high-spouting whale who lives on a hill
And who never comes down 'til it's time to refill.
On Beyond Zebra
Dr. Suess

An example of all four types of comic language is found in a conversation between the characters of Jack and Algernon in Oscar Wilde's play, *The Importance of Being Earnest:*

Jack: ...Her mother is a gorgon...I don't *Sarcasm*
    really know what a gorgon is like, but
    I'm quite sure that Lady Bracknell is *Absurdity*
    one. I beg your pardon Algy, I suppose
    I shouldn't talk about your own aunt
    that way before you.

Algernon: My dear boy, I love hearing my
    relations abused. It is the only
    thing that makes me put up with them
    at all. Relations are simply a tedious
    pack of people who haven't the remotest *Sarcasm*
    knowledge of how to live, nor the smallest
    instinct about when to die. By the way,
    did you tell Gwendolyn the truth about
    your being Ernest in town and Jack in
    the country?

Jack: My dear fellow, the truth isn't quite
    the sort of thing one tells a nice sweet
    refined girl. ...I am sick to death of *Repartee*
    cleverness. Everybody is clever now-
    adays. You can't go anywhere without
    meeting clever people. The thing has

become an absolute public nuisance. I
wish to goodness we had a few fools left. *Irony*

The humor of language is the surest indicator of higher thinking. In no other form of communication is so much thought needed. The best humor requires some amount of thought to understand. Having to think a bit to comprehend a joke makes the laughter more rewarding. Having to contemplate while creating a joke makes the experience of delivering it more rewarding. Because language requires a higher level of thinking, laughter at language is a wonderful prize no matter what stage you're on, or in. At least that's what I think I meant to say.

Chapter 6
IMITATION

"See if you recognize this one..."

Where would comedians be if people hadn't developed a love for imitating each other? There is no better way to simultaneously make people laugh and cut another person down to size than by imitating that person. Especially if you add a touch of exaggeration to bring out their most goofy qualities. Imagine the cave-man, Forg, who couldn't establish himself well in his tribe. He had no strength or fighting ability and was lousy at hunting. Forg was frustrated and helpless. He wanted to be in good standing with the tribe, but he was no match for the leader, Brok. Brok could beat two men at once. He always got first pick of the day's kill and his choice of women in the tribe. Forg's frustration was compounded by the fact that he had talents—no one could imitate the call of the bull moose during a hunt better than he. When he put on a bear skin and danced around the fire, everyone was in stitches, even though they didn't know what stitches were yet. His talents were noticed and appreciated, but not highly valued. After all, what good was dancing around in a bear skin when you were hungry?

To make matters worse, Brok was not even all that smart. "Heck," thought Forg, "Brok is so stupid, he tried barbecuing a tree branch to see if it made good lunch." No one in the tribe dared call attention to Brok's stupidity because of his awesome strength. One day, Forg was walking through the cave and a rock fell and hit him on the head. This jarred something loose in his skull and he got a brilliant idea. "Don't fight Brok on his ground," he thought to himself, "Make him fight you on yours." Better yet, be clever and win without fighting." So, Forg gathered up all of the leader's bear skins and put them on at the next tribe meeting. He started strutting around like Brok, copying his voice and movements exactly, but with a little sarcastic flair. This had everyone laughing uproariously, including Brok, who wasn't even smart enough to realize that he was the butt of the joke. He thought Forg had created a new way of honoring him. Forg was lucky that Brok wasn't keen enough to see the insult, or Forg would've been the next trophy on Brok's cave wall. Forg had established a new standing in the tribe, and he didn't have to get all sweaty and hunt dangerous animals to do it.

It's remarkable how comedians and playwrights have had to dance around the issue of politics and power when using the humor of imitation. Not enough sarcasm, and the people you are trying to entertain will think you are too timid and middle-of-the-road. They want to see famous and important people cut down to size, and they want the insult to sting hard. The common man is tired of cowering in front of the elite, so he likes to see those arrogant snobs drilled on stage by a witty performer. In days of old if the writer or comedian went too far however, and his impressions hit a little too close to home, the powers that be may find the piece a bit too insulting. If the person being skewered was in a position of extreme power this could be dangerous for the performer. Luckily, times have changed.

The comedy of imitation falls into two areas: impression and mimicry. Impressions are imitations of famous or well-known people. Usually the impression contains some sort of exaggeration of either a physical or verbal characteristic. In order for the comedy of impressions to work, the audience must be familiar with the subject.

I would like to do an impression for you now. "Hey you guys, let's play some football." That's a kid from my hometown. Nobody ever recognizes that one.

Dean Johnson, Minneapolis comedian

Mr. Johnson, in the above example, points the joke back on himself by trying to perform a character that we not only don't know, but wouldn't care to see on stage even if we did know him. This is where a good many comedians find trouble when they first make the leap from being the funny character at parties to the professional comedian. It's easy to make your family laugh by imitating Uncle Bob bowling. Everybody knows Uncle Bob and it doesn't take much imagination for them to him in your impression. The family likes Uncle Bob and good-natured ribbing is part of many families, so everyone is ready to laugh. Get the comedian on stage however, and the audience sits wondering who Uncle Bob is.

Some comedians try impressions of famous people only to find out that, while their impression is a perfect copy of the real thing, no one cares enough about the real thing to laugh. In order for impressions to work, not only must they be an accurate depiction of the famous person, but there must be something about the famous person worth copying. The copying can take place on different levels, from a simple imitation of the victim's voice or gestures, to clever exaggerations of key elements of the person's character. Many comedians select subjects for imitation not so much for their social significance, but for the ease in finding characteristics to copy—Richard Nixon's low gravely voice, James Stewart's stuttering delivery, Johnny Carson's nasal laugh and finger-to-the-upper-lip gesture.

Many famous people have characteristics that are so strange that some comedians think all they need to do is display the trait on stage for a laugh. This will often fail because of an old comedy axiom: you can't parody that which parodies itself. If the audience has already recognized an oddity about a famous person, they don't need a comedian pointing it out. Instead they want a comedian who can go one step further and surprise them with something they hadn't noticed.

Truly accomplished performers will develop caricature-like impressions of everyone in the public eye. These comedians must dig deeper than the average "I can do John Wayne and Jack

Nicholson" performer. They must examine every detail of voice and movement of their subject and select for the stage those details that are unique. Rich Little became famous by not satisfying himself with the impressions he was comfortable with; rather he created characters for almost every political figure, movie star, singer, and entertainer that the audience could possibly know.

Mimicry, the other type of imitation, involves performing a rendition of a person the audience is not familiar with, but can recognize from their own life. If the guy doing a great job of Uncle Bob bowling were to perform it on stage effectively enough that, even though we don't know Uncle Bob personally, we can recognize the character, it would be funny. For mimicry to be funny, we must either know someone similar to the character, or recognize the type of person being portrayed. In either case, there is a strong sense of recognition needed to create laughter.

When telling a story about my mother, I often slip into an exaggerated copy of her voice. The audience doesn't know my mother, but they can recognize the common characteristics between my mother and theirs. When you get right down to it, most mothers sound the same anyway. When I refer to my father, out comes his voice, posture, and attitude. The same for everyone in my family. A story told this way becomes its own little play, with each character in the story given a distinct voice and manner of movement. We imagine people from our own lives in the situation depicted by the comedian.

Jonathan Winters packed his performances with incredible mimicry. A master at voices, he stayed away from imitating famous people, choosing instead to treat us to a parade of our own family, friends, co-workers, and selves. Through his mimicry we could see the stupidity of our actions. I almost didn't include his routine below, "The Deer Hunters," because ink on a page can never equal the delight of hearing his many voices. Use your imagination.

[Hunter #1]: *Ed. Listen, do me a favor. Now listen to me. This year, doggonit we're gonna get a deer. Last year we just fooled around in the cottage and got sauced. And we didn't accomplish anything for a week. Let's get a deer, huh? It's no fun coming back with a half a bear, and some dead trout. Let's get a deer this year, come on. And I want you to stay on that spot. You promise? All right, well, just stay there. (Calls to dog) Chick! Chick!*
BLAM!
#1: *Oh gees. Joe you shot Chick already. We haven't been out 15 minutes. I'm sorry Chick. Chick's dead. Put him on the bumper. Tom, now I want you down in the gully, you understand?*
[Tom]: *Listen, there wasn't nothing down there last year. Wasn't anything, but dried leaves.*
#1: *Well believe me we never know...*
BLAM!

#1: *What was that? Ralph. Ralph, why would you shoot him in the tree? He was climbing up there to get a sight of the valley. Come on down.*

THUNK.

BLAM!

#1: *What was that? Tom's already dead. Now, there you go, that's what I mean. That's what I mean by not staying on your spot.*

BLAM!

#1: *What was that now? Now Ralph's dead. Ralph you shouldn't 'a been walking through that area there. Are you dead Ralph?*

[Ralph]: *Oooooh! Oooooh!*

#1: *Well, somebody put him on the bumper then, 'cause I want to take something back this year.*

Jonathan Winters

"Jonathan Winter...Wings It!"

The laughter at impressions and mimicry come from two different sources: the imitation of a familiar character and the statements made about the person through the imitation. The laughter from comments about the character could stem from a sense of sarcasm or satire (chapter 8). The laughter from the imitation is its own source. Whether the comedian actually makes statements about the character or not, we delight in seeing people copied by others. Many of the exaggerated characteristics displayed by comedians are mannerisms that we all have, so when we laugh at the comedian we are actually laughing at our own shortcomings. An interesting form of imitation is often used in developing characters for science fiction. In both versions of the Star Trek television series, "Star Trek" and "Star Trek: The Next Generation," we see characters who represent one single element of humanity. The element that is one small part of our being is separated and made the dominant characteristic in the science fiction character. The character of Spock exaggerates the logical side of people, Worf (from "The Next Generation") exaggerates hostility and aggression, Data represents curiosity, Captain Kirk is brash, and every female love interest for Captain Kirk was sensuality played to such a high degree that it was almost comical.

Impressions display the characteristics that are not only common to all of us, but that are represented singularly in famous people. We all stammer at times while thinking of what to say, but James Stewart takes it to an extreme that few people match. Impressions of famous people serve to bring larger-than-life characters down to size, evening the playing field of life for us common folks.

Imitation causes laughter for a number of reasons, and like most forms of comedy, combines the effects of more than one level of the pyramid. Actor and comedian Jim Carey is noted for his amazing rubber-faced impressions of famous TV and movie stars. While most impressionists concentrate on copying the star's voice, Carey spent most of his youth perfecting control of his facial muscles. He is actually able to re-create the star's face by contorting his own. Adding the voice becomes the frosting on the cake (or icing, depending on where you grew up). Laughter at imitation, especially the multi-leveled face-body-and-voice, is caused by our delight in seeing or hearing an entirely different person portrayed by the comedian. Carey's expressions and gestures also cause laughter of physical comedy. We laugh both at the imitation and the wild physicality he employs. Any statements he makes about the person he is imitating, whether direct or by simple virtue of the imitation, are akin to satire. Imitation also carries with it an element of the next chapter, "Character Contradiction." (Maybe I should have written this book in reverse so the things I say at the beginning would make sense because of what I say at the end.)

Chapter 7
CHARACTER CONTRADICTION

*"Who would have thought a guy like him
would do a thing like that?"*

When we see characters in a play, a comedy act, or in real life, we see patterns in their behavior. After a while we learn to expect certain types of behavior from them in particular situations. We do this unconsciously because it helps us keep a sense of order in our life. Expectations help smooth out our daily routine, otherwise we would approach everyday like an infant, Having to relearn everything and stumble through life one step at a time. In fact, a major function of the brain is to fill in missing information so that we may understand our surroundings. When people read a book they don't actually look at every word, that would be tedious and our reading speed would be that of a second-grader. Instead, the brain causes the eye to skip over the sentences while it makes assumptions as to the content.

The brain is able to make assumptions based on past experiences. The same assumptions are made automatically everyday as we encounter different situations. If we were to see an old woman sitting on a park bench with a grocery cart next to her filled with aluminum cans, our assumption would be based on our experiences. If we had just driven through a poor part of town, we would assume she was a homeless woman. If we had just finished watching a commercial about senior citizens gathering aluminum cans to recycle for charity, we would assume instead that she was a retiree helping at a local center.

Our tendency to expect specific behaviors and attitudes from others grows stronger the more we know the person. Since the brain responds to surprise with laughter, if people unexpectedly break out of the pattern we assume of them, we laugh.

Laughter of character contradiction can be seen on stage and in everyday life. We see it when a staunch priest walking down the street suddenly jumps into a little girls' game of jump rope, when a little old lady sees a good looking man walk by and she says, "Hey joy-chops, what a body!", or when a graceful ballet teacher trips on the way into a classroom. Everyday life produces many laughs from character contradiction, because people so easily fall out of character. We expect our friend in the restaurant to act normally and eat a meal, so it would come as a surprise if halfway during the meal he or she started singing a Broadway showtune using the sandwich as a microphone.

Since comedians are trying to make us laugh, we are a bit wary about their actions right from the start. To overcome this suspicion a comedian must lull the viewer into a false sense of normalcy, then when the viewer has developed normal expectations, the comedian breaks out of character. This explains why many novice stand-up comedians find it easy to be funny to their friends, and yet be boring to an audience of strangers. When these hopeful funny people go to the bar with a group of friends and break into a funny voice or an odd walk, their friends are on the floor with laughter. Then they try the same thing in a comedy club and the crowd starts gathering their coats. The humor these people are trying to employ relies on their audience knowing them, which is easy with a group of friends.

Many amateur performers also fail because they develop material that relies on the audience being familiar with the subject in the story, which of course they are not. "So Uncle Bob spit on the duck! He spit on it! Isn't that funny? I guess you had to be there...." (We have a saying in comedy, "If you had to be there, the joke ain't funny!")

The laughter of character contradiction can be heightened if the performer gives the impression that he or she is unaware of the inconsistency of character. If an old lady winked at us just before wildly jumping in a wading pool, we would know that she was aware of her actions. We would get the sense that she was trying to make us laugh and the humor would be gone. In many ways, character contradiction requires the same element for laughter as storyline—*the audience is aware of something that the character in the story is not.*

Any situation can be seen as its own story. Take any moment out of your life and pretend someone was watching it on TV. To them, your life is a story. You are a character and you are expected to behave in a certain manner. Viewers take great delight in seeing you bumble around and unknowingly fall out of character. This pleasure is based on the fact that, even though you know you might be acting out of character for yourself, *you don't realize it's funny.* If you let on that you know you're acting funny, the person watching the story of your life is not in on something secret and will not laugh. If you were to give the impression that you knew you were acting out of character, the audience may still laugh because of the reactions of those around you, but their laughter is no longer caused by character contradiction. Laughter in this case would be at the physical manifestation of their surprise, so it would be laughter of physical comedy. Good comedians always give the impression that they are unaware that anything odd has happened. Being "in on the joke" is a necessary element for an audience to laugh at any of the seven levels of comedy.

Laughter at character contradiction depends on the audience's ability to observe societal norms and create expectations based on experience. This need for the audience to be able to observe others and discern patterns of behavior places the comedy of character contradiction high on the pyramid of comedy.

There is another reason people laugh at someone who steps out of character. People laugh at someone not only because he or she appears absentminded, but because that person has stepped outside of normal society. Laughter is as much criticism as it is praise, and when a contradiction of character reveals that someone has fallen outside of society's bounds, our laughter is a means of pushing them back in. Our laughter at someone's *unsociability* is actually a means of control.

Mike Nichols and Elaine May were a comedy duo that grew out of the Compass Theatre, a precursor to The Second City in Chicago in the late '50s. Nichols and May became so popular as part of the Compass troupe that they struck out on their own and landed on Broadway with a show that would go on to win critical and popular acclaim, <u>An Evening with Mike Nichols and Elaine May</u>. One of their routines, *Mother and Son*, demonstrates character contradiction in sketch form. The conversation takes on a comical air when you realize that the mother is not just talking to her son, but that he is a NASA rocket scientist. While reading the routine you must imagine a son that is controlled and henpecked by a domineering mother. Every word out of her mouth is meant to fill him with guilt. He is forever apologizing for "not being a good son."

Phone rings, Arthur answers.
Hello.
Hello Arthur? This is your mother. **Do you remember me?**
Mom! Hi! I was just going to call you is that a funny thing...
Arthur?
...you know that I had my hand on the phone, to call....

Arthur, you were supposed to call me last Friday.

Mother, darling, I just didn't have a second and I could cut my throat....

You didn't have a second?

...I was so busy....

Arthur, I sat by that phone all day Friday.

It was just work, work, work....

All day Friday night.

And darling, I kept thinking, "I gotta call Mom."

And all day Saturday.

Listen, believe me....

All day Sunday. And your father said to me, "Phyllis, eat something, you'll faint." I said, "No Harry no, I don't want my mouth to be full when my son calls me." You never called.

Mom, I was sending up Vanguard (A rocket in the '60s), *I didn't have a second.*

(Long pause from mother) *Well, it's always something isn't it?*

Okay mom....

You know Arthur, I'm sure that all the other scientists there have mothers. And I'm sure that they all find time, after their breakfast or before their count-off...

Down.

...to pick up a phone and call their mother. And you know how I worry. I read in the paper how you keep losing them.

Mother! I don't lose them!

Well I nearly went out of my mind.

Okay honey now put....

I thought, what if they're taking it out of his pay?

Mike Nichols and Elaine May
An Evening with Mike Nichols and Elaine May

There are, of course, times when we delight in someone's eccentricities and laugh to applaud that person for breaking out of the norm in a delightful way. We love to see rebels challenge authority, mainly because we don't have the guts to do it ourselves. So we will laugh to cheer individuality and spunk. In the play, *Tartuffe*, by the French playwright Moliere, the main character is a priest who acts very unpriest-like. In the course of the play he propositions another man's wife, attempts to embezzle the man's estate, and almost marries the man's daughter. At the beginning of the play we laugh at the wildly uncharacteristic behavior of the priest, yet after we become accustomed to the man's behavior, we are no longer surprised when he acts inappropriately, so our laughter changes because we learn to expect his actions. We begin to identify with Tartuffe's desires, and we applaud with laughter his outrageous behavior.

Character Contradiction is a form of humor that is often easier for the actor than for the stand-up comedian. Comedians are only in front of an audience for a short time. The audience has very little time to form expectations of the comedians behavior, so almost any action or word may seem within the parameters of his or her character. In fact, because we know the comedian is going to try to make us laugh, we expect much more outlandish behavior than normal. A professional speaker addressing a group of executives may get a laugh by delivering a relatively weak joke, while the same joke would get no response when delivered by a comedian. Our expectations are markedly different in each situation. This is why many people who can make their friends and co-workers laugh try stand-up comedy only to discover it is much more difficult than it looks.

Effective performers develop a persona that remains constant throughout their act, so when they occasionally act out of character they have ensured that the audience will be surprised and they will be rewarded with laughter. Johnny Carson used this to great success on *The Tonight Show*. As host of the show he remained congenial and warm, welcoming guests and engaging in harmless chit-chat. Every now and then he would have a guest that was out of the ordinary, a zookeeper for instance, and suddenly we would see the cool and collected Johnny Carson sitting calmly while a bird poops on his head. Sometimes Johnny himself would perform in a comedy sketch that would break him out of character. One character of his, "The Amazing Carnak," had Carson dressed in an outlandish turban and cape, psychically answering questions from his partner, Ed McMahon. Remember of course, the laughter of character contradiction only applies when you are surprised at uncharacteristic behavior. After seeing The Amazing Carnak repeatedly, the laughter would have to be generated from the actual material in the sketch.

Developing a strong, recognizable character is necessary for all good comedic performers, and important if you want to take advantage of character contradiction. Just don't have a bird poop on your head like Carson. It's messy and the bit has been done to death.

Chapter 8
SATIRE

No doubt, just as watchmakers provide a particularly good
movement with a similarly valuable case, so it may happen
with jokes that the best achievements in the way of jokes are
used as an envelope for thoughts of the greatest substance.
Sigmund Freud

"I laughed 'til I cried"
The Frogs, Aristophanes

We have now reached the highest level of comedy. Satire
calls upon the audience to make the most complex mental
associations, to do the most brain work to understand the
humor. It is the comedy of ideas, the comedy of thought. All
comedy is thought-provoking, but satire goes further, it makes
a judgment. Simply defined, satire is comedy that *compares*
the world the way it is with the way it ought to be. It forces us
to review the morals and ideals by which we govern our lives.
In satire, the comedian holds aspects of our lives up to ridicule.
We now laugh *with* as much as *at.*

The object of satirical ridicule may be as grandiose as politics
and religion or as common as the neighborhood trash collector.

As long as the comedian is saying that something isn't the way it ought to be, he is employing satire. People often mistake sarcasm for satire, and the differences are subtle. However while a satirical statement may be made sarcastically, not all sarcasm is satire. In general terms, sarcasm is directed at a single individual, while satire concerns a broader social issue. If a comedian talks about how bad a particular bus driver was on a recent bus trip, she is being sarcastic. If she talks about the sorry state of buses in general, or the mass transit system as a whole, she is making a satirical comment. If she uses one bus driver to make a point about all bus drivers, satire is again at work.

In many other forms of comedy the comedian is dropped to a level below the audience, acting silly and out of control. In satire the audience and the comedian bond together to criticize an outside entity. Satire is borne of discontent. When we laugh at satire, we voice our agreement at the comedians admonishment of the world. It is as if the audience is laughing for no other reason than to show their support for a criticism made by the speaker.

Before his acting talents were put to use on television, Bob Newhart began his career in stand-up comedy. His style of comedy was almost solely based on social satire, but it was not of the malicious kind that other, more blunt, comedians use. This is evident in his routine, "Nobody Will Ever Play Baseball." Below, in a style created by Newhart, we hear the inventor of Baseball, Abner Doubleday, trying to convince an administrator that his new game would be perfect for the Olympics.

Administrator: *Hello, Olympic Games. What can I do for you Mr. Doubleday? You've got a game. How many couples? Eighteen people? That's a lot of people. Well the ideal game is two, three couples come over to the house, they get a little smashed and you know. You can't play it in the house either? See, you got two things right there against you. All right, all right, tell me about it. You got nine guys on each side, yeah. And you got a pitcher and a catcher, and they throw this ball back and forth. And that's all there is to it? All right, a guy from the other side stands between 'em. With a bat. I see. And he just watches them? Oh I see, he swings at it. He may or he may not swing at it. Depending on what? If it looked like it were a ball. (pause) Ah, what's a ball Mr. Doubleday? You got this plate, uh huh. And as long as it's above the knees (starts to giggle), but below the shoulders (laughing), no go ahead, I'm listening, it's a strike. Three strikes and you're out. And three balls...not three balls, four balls (giggling some more). Why four balls Mr. Doubleday? Nobody's ever asked you before? If he hits it, what happens? He runs as far as he can...before somebody catches it. As long as it stays what? As long as it stays fair. And what's fair Mr. Doubleday? You've got these two white lines. Is... is this a rib? Is this one of the guys in the office?*

Bob Newhart
"The Button-Down Mind of Bob Newhart"

102

Satire, through the safe means of laughter, can make us take a step back and examine our behavior. It has the unique power to instigate change in society. During the Vietnam war, when the country's loyalties and politics were divided, comedians did much to voice what they thought was the hypocrisy of our nation's involvement in the war. Satire is much more effective than preaching or debate in swaying public opinion. This is because of its slyly derisive nature. If you simply argue your point of view with someone, you give them the option to disagree. It is easy for them to say you're nuts, that you don't know what you're talking about. Both of you leave the debate thinking the other is wrong, but neither has really gained the upper hand. This lets your opponent leave with his dignity intact, and no one really wants that in an argument (at least no one who's married). If, however, as you debate, you cause others to laugh at your opponent, this public ridicule causes much more reconsideration on your opponent's part. It is one thing to have someone tell you you're wrong; it is quite another to have people laugh in your face. There is no retort to a flat-out guffaw in the face. Any attempt the part of the target to regain control is futile. If you are being laughed at and you respond with anger, you look out of control and weak. If you respond with debate, you look like a stuffed-shirt who can't take a joke. Either way you come out behind. Laughter carries so much more sting than logic.

When pointed in the right direction, satire can be used for social control. Politicians know that if they simply disagree with an opponent, they only create unresolved conflict. The voters are left to decide for themselves who is right. If they can smash their opponent's dignity by satirically ripping apart opposing viewpoints, the laughter of ridicule seals their victory. In the British parliament, sarcastic satire is a common and powerful weapon. In the United States congress, insults and cutting remarks take a backseat to passionate rhetoric and driving debate. In Great Britain, politicians use a healthy mixture of satire, sarcasm, repartee, and outright insult to attack their opponent's position. As spectators and fellow parliament members eagerly observe, two opposing "benches" engage in a verbal swordfight no less deadly than the real thing (at least to their careers). In fact, as tradition dictates, the two opposing sides are today still kept at a distance equal to two swordlengths. Verbal swordplay is necessary because of the premium given in Britain to wit and intelligence. We value intelligence in America too, but we prefer down-to-earth knowledge or "everyman" sarcasm. We like someone who "speaks from the gut." If someone's witty remarks use too high-minded a vocabulary, we feel no sense of camaraderie. We are more likely to side with the defender of such remarks. The use of "ten-dollar words" can make an outsider of the common person.

Wit and polish in public speaking is important for Lords of the House. If a well-spoken gentleman unseats his opponent with wit and satire, he displays his superior character and intellect. It's almost as if he were saying, "I don't need to resort to fisticuffs with you, you swine. I can match you wit for wit." This sort of politician garners support, even if the followers aren't quite sure of his cause (a phenomenon not foreign to the US). Sometimes the insults in the House of Lords border on the cheap and childish. This, however draws scorn from the lady Speaker of the House, who has been known to say, "We have such a rich vocabulary at our disposal, to resort to vulgar attack is unnecessary." It is fun to witness the Lords arguing because, no matter how insulting the remark made about an opposing politician, the gentleman is always referred to as, "The Right Honorable...." It seems that one must follow decorum even when engaged in mudslinging. I wonder if it hurts less to be called a 'right honorable' jerk?

We live in satirical luxury today. In other times and other countries, freedom of expression meant little, and comedy of satire suffered for it. In monarchies of old, where it was forbidden to speak out against the king or queen, comedy remained a very base and childish style of theatre, relying heavily on physical humor and simple characters. Those that chose to criticize the leaders of the day did so at their own great risk. Moliere, whom we spoke of in the previous chapter, "Character Contradiction," was a master at creating satire, even though his every worked was under a microscope. Born in France, 1622 as Jean-Baptiste Poquelin, he took the stage name, Moliere, when he started acting and writing (see, even then they had egos). To this day no one knows where he got the name Moliere.

In seventeenth century France, plays were performed for the aristocracy and peasants at the same time. The peasants would watch the play from the floor while the bourgeois sat in balcony seats. Moliere knew that he had to please both sides of society, the rabble in the pit *and* the aristocracy in the balcony. To do so would mean making fun of the peasants for the pleasure of the aristocrats, and vice versa. The peasants wanted to see bawdy humor, but also an occasional stab at the big-wigs. The aristocrats wanted to see interesting plots in which their egos were stroked. It was easy to please the aristocrats, just make peasant characters look like fools and keep a lively plot going. Peasants however, would not sit still for a play that pandered to the very royalty that kept them oppressed. Moliere needed to satirize the foibles of high society, but if he made the satire too obvious he would be in very real danger. In old France, if a line in a play seemed to insult the aristocracy, the actor and playwright might be thrown in jail and stripped of all chattel. If the insurrection was severe enough, the offending writer would be beheaded. So, he had the dilemma of pleasing the lower class, who made up the bulk of his audience, and the upper class, who made up the bulk of his money.

Moliere was able to craft plays that had characters representing both peasant and ruler. The rulers in the plays were stupid, slow-witted, and always on the losing end of the battle. The peasants seemed outwardly as foolish, but always managed to come out ahead. The characters were so finely written that the aristocracy never caught on that they were the brunt of the joke. In their eyes, the upper class characters in the play were respectable society folk who were victims of circumstance. Often, they were so busy laughing at the stabs made at peasants that they didn't see what was being said about them. The peasants in the audience could see that it was the peasants that got the upper hand in the play by letting the rulers think they had won. Both audiences went home laughing, thinking the other had been made fools.

It is not surprising that the peasants were able to see the deception and enjoy it among themselves. Every oppressed people must, by necessity, become adept at sensing the mood of their oppressor. It is a tool of survival to know when to attend closely to your master and when to make yourself scarce. This is true for people in many situations. Women and children in abusive relationships report that they become very skilled at sensing whether the husband or father is in a good or bad mood. They know just when to speak or when to steer clear. Years of living in a similar environment trained the peasants to pick up on nuances that the upper class missed, which is ironic considering it was the upper class who thought that the peasants were too ignorant to catch the meaning of the play. A look at some of Moliere's play titles shows the obvious target of the satire: *The Blunderer, The Jealous Prince, The School for Husbands, The Bores, The Hypocrite, The Imaginary Invalid,* and *The Great Booby of a Son as Foolish as his Father.* I think the last title would make a good sit-com.

Before we think of how stupid the people of the seventeenth century were for needing such obvious titles, we should remember the titles of some of our own movies: *The Jerk, Dumb and Dumber, Grumpy Old Men,* and *Meatballs.* Sometimes an obvious description of the show is the best way to market it to the public. The fact that Moliere was able to continue the charade for so long attests to his genius. Imagine the satirists of our day—Bill Maher, George Carlin, Lenny Bruce, Will Durst, Jay Leno, and David Letterman—if they knew that a step over the line would cost them their career, their possessions, and even their head.

Freud believed that part of the reason for laughter at satire stems from the unconscious mind. He links many forms of laughter to past experiences that are buried in our memories. Freud reasoned that the audience laughs at satire because satire depicts situations of misfortune, and the audience recollects similar situations in their own lives. In some cases, satire is recalling bad experiences for the audience in a humorous setting, allowing them to laugh at their painful memories, thereby dealing with the memories positively. Some satire carries with it bluntness and tenacity, much like the jungle fight and the resulting victory cry. Other forms are subtle, like a wolf in sheep's skin. We laugh at the satirical statement, and because the we are able to see through the disguise and the target of the satire can't.

"It is impossible to carry the torch of truth through a crowd without singeing someone's beard"
G.C. von Lichtenberg, 1853

The above statement by the German philosopher Lichtenburg brings up one of the most controversial elements of satire, that of social good taste. Satire often walks the line of what society would consider acceptable or unacceptable humor. In order to really be satirical, to make statements about what is wrong with society, one must step on a few toes. Consider the jokes below and see which are satirical and which simply rely on shock value for laughter.

Joke #1 (a popular joke in America after shootings occurred in several post offices)
"What does it mean when the post office flies its flag at half mast?"
"They're hiring."

Joke #2
A guy came home to find his girlfriend packing a suitcase. He asked, "What are you doing?"
"I'm leaving," she replied. "Someone told me you are a pedophile!"
"Pedophile!" he exclaimed. "That's a pretty big word for an eight-year-old."

Joke #3
Did you hear about the time Jesus walked into a hotel, put three nails on the counter and asked, "Can you put me up for the night?"

These jokes are the type that instantly divide people. Some people would not only refuse to laugh at them, but they would criticize anyone else for laughing. Some people would laugh at first, and feel embarrassed later. Others would laugh out loud and say to those who complain, "Come on, it's only a joke!" Your ability to laugh depends on your background and personal experiences. Of the third joke about Jesus, people who follow a strict religion might consider it blasphemy. The fear of eternal damnation can be quite a deterrent to laughter.

I have heard it said, many times, "Lighten up! God is the one who gave us a sense of humor in the first place." I prefer Voltaire's quote, *"God is a comedian playing to an audience who is afraid to laugh."* To observe the jokes objectively however, one must remember that satire requires a social statement. A joke may be funny, but to be satirical it must do more than shock the listener—it must offer an opinion. So, the joke about Jesus is not satirical, since it does not provide a statement about either Jesus or Christianity. It merely shocks the listener and provides an unusual pairing of a historical event in a modern day setting.

The second joke about the eight-year-old girlfriend treads on very dangerous ground. Pedophilia is not only a crime, it is also one of our most heinous social taboos. Some would say however, that the joke offers more than just shock value. It offers a perspective on the reality of pedophilia. The joke illuminates the fact that many young people who are victims of pedophilia are not even old enough to be aware that it is wrong. The fact that this joke appears now as opposed to years ago illustrates the way society treats delicate issues. Twenty years ago no one dared speak of date rape in public; now it is a regular part of sex education in high schools and universities. It is a short step from speaking about sensitive issues to joking about them. The kind of jokes a society enjoys, or allows, are a barometer for the issues of the day.

In order for a social wrong to be stopped, it must be brought into the open. It must become part of people's conversation so misconceptions can be erased. This has helped us more effectively deal with such issues as sexual diversity, physical diversity, race, alternative lifestyles, and cultural differences. In the grand tradition of all comedy, comedians seek to educate as well as amuse, the result is greater social awareness without all the preaching you get at church.

The first joke about the post office is an obvious satirical comment on the rash of shootings committed by postal workers in the early '90s. It is a very simple statement, offering the opinion that the postal service has far too many dangerous personalities. Jokes such as these are common among comedians, and they have a certain importance in our culture. When people see news reports of violence and destruction they feel shock and sadness, but the feeling is a private one. Comedy provides people an opportunity to share their anger about issues in a public forum. A group laugh gives people the chance to, as a collective, thumb their nose at the people or institutions that disgust them, and the presence of laughter makes the thumb a relatively harmless one. Such a gathering would certainly not remain as non-destructive if a bunch of people instead got together in a park and started screaming and yelling about the state of the world. Just ask the survivors of the Los Angeles riots.

Comedy has a way of being a safe haven to talk about subjects that can't be broached in normal conversation. With this freedom, some comedians come right out and say, "All right, we're going to talk about some uncomfortable stuff. So if ya want to leave now ya better go!" A young comedian starting out at Stevie Ray's comedy theatre & cabaret in the early 90's knew this and wanted to take advantage of it. She told me that she noticed a lot of comedians of the day used humor to expose the audience to new ways of thinking and different lifestyles. Gays were using comedy to show audiences what being gay was like, and that they were not so different from the rest of the world. While interviewing for my comedy class she said she wanted to use stand-up as a way to give the audience a glimpse of her life as a transsexual. She would start her act by putting the audience at ease with laughter.

"Hey everybody! My names xxxxx and I'm a transsexual. (long pause) *Well, I don't hear any shotguns loading so I guess it's safe to go on."*

By showing the she understood the uncomfortable nature of the subject, the comedian was able to relax the audience and forewarn them of material that might be shocking.

Satire places great importance on the indirect nature of comedy, believing that, while audiences will laugh at direct attacks at people and events, they will *appreciate* the comedy even more if they must work to find the insult. The more difficult the mental association, the more rewarding the laugh. This follows human nature in that we appreciate all things more when we must work to achieve them (except when it comes to sex or chocolate).

Part II
THE BODY AND BRAIN OF LAUGHING

Chapter 9
THE PHYSIOLOGY OF LAUGHTER

"She who laughs, lasts"
A bumper sticker I saw on a car.

We have now investigated all the levels of comedy. We have seen how, as a person matures his or her ability to appreciate different forms of comedy changes. The levels of the pyramid explain the different forms of comedy, but they do not explain why laughter exists in the first place. Every level on the pyramid has a corresponding real-life situation. Physical comedy: someone falling on the ice; Obscenity: someone swearing; Storyline: someone involved in a chase, and so on. However, if you see someone fall on the ice it is just as likely you would react with concern as with laughter. There are many times when we are aware of impending doom for a character in a story, but do not express ourselves by laughing. What conditions must be present to make sure the situations represented in the seven levels of comedy result in laughter rather than anger, fear, or rage? There are reasons why we respond with one emotion over another. A good comedian knows how to craft the situation so that the response is always laughter.

By outward appearances, laughter doesn't seem to accomplish anything, so it is hard to imagine how it would have evolved as a means of communication in a higher form of animal like humans. The appendix in our colon does nothing for us, but at least we know that at one time it had a function. So its present useless condition is excused as a phase of evolution between usefulness and complete omission. Laughter must serve a very useful purpose to have evolved into something we use everyday. Scientists have only recently discovered just how dependent we are on laughter for mental and physical health. Indeed, our need for laughter has its basis in our psychology and our physiology.

Sigmund Freud had a few ideas about the psychological basis for laughter. He believed the formula for laughter included the appearance of criticism. The comedian presents the facade that a criticism is about to be made, and the listener knows that the result of the criticism will be a tense atmosphere. This expectation creates a build up of tension in the listener. When the criticism is revealed to be a joke, the result is laughter that releases the pent-up psychological tension. Freud also goes on to speculate that laughter occurs because of a lessening of "psychical energy." The connections jokes make between different subjects lessens the amount of brain work needed on the part of the listener to comprehend the idea, and the result is laughter. The brain expects to do a certain amount of work in

115

relation to a thought or idea, and when the work unexpectedly turns out to be less, the excess brain activity, or "psychical energy" is released much like a safety valve opening. Perhaps this "psychical energy" is the reason why people give a short laugh when they discover that a box is much lighter than they thought and they can lift it with unexpected ease. This goes against the notion that the brain delights in making intricate connections and expresses delight with laughter. There are many types of laughter for different forms of comedy, so perhaps the two theories can co-exist. In either case, the act of laughter is a release of mental tension, and therefore a healthy activity.

Laughter is indeed one of the few physical acts that preserve mental health. If tension and stress is to be released from the body and mind, it can only be accomplished through an outpouring of emotion or physical energy. Other strong emotions such as crying and screaming do relieve stress, but they're not as much fun as laughter. Physical exertion... exercise, sports, sex, active hobbies...release physical energy, but you can't play a quick round of racquetball when you're feeling tense at the office. And with our competitive nature, some physical endeavors leave us more tense than when we started. Laughter is an immediate, pleasant, risk-free stress reliever.

Studies have shown that laughter is the most common response to something as common as a friend walking into a room where a group of people are gathered. It's no accident that we react so often and so easily with laughter. Laughter is such a quick and effective tool for providing mental and physical health, the brain has simply acted to promote its own survival by developing an automatic response. It's as if the brain said, *"I don't trust you to do this on your own. So, like breathing and blinking, I'm taking over. You just watch professional wrestling and leave me alone."*

Laughter is also extremely important as a means of social interaction. People have needed social contact since before man walked upright. At first we banded in groups to more effectively fend off attackers and protect our family, tribe, and possessions. Then we learned to stick together because we could produce more food in teams than on our own. Now we recognize the need to interact for companionship and affection. We derive much of our self-esteem from the approval of our peers. Social gatherings justify our self-worth, solidify ideals and philosophies, and provide us with a mental safety net, instead of just the physical net we needed while hunting as primitives. Laughter is a more positive means of social interaction than any other activity. Some would say dancing is just as positive, but I've seen some people dance, I'm sticking to my theory.

Other social events require either aggression, as in tournaments and games, or physical and mental skill, as in sports or dancing. Laughter brings people together in a completely non-competitive arena. Even if the laughter is the result of competitive repartee, the atmosphere is still light-hearted and the competition disappears during the actual act of laughter. Laughter most often occurs when there are at least two people present. You may simply chuckle at a funny television show while sitting at home alone, but watch the same show with a group of friends and you'll howl with laughter. As William Shakespeare said in *Love's Labour's Lost:*

A jest's prosperity lies in the ear
of him that hears it, never in the tongue
of him that makes it....

Since laughter is enhanced by being in a group, people will seek out others with whom to laugh. The human mind has developed a function that, in the same act, promotes health and ensures social interaction.

We have all heard that laughter is contagious, and this is more physically true than you might expect. If you stand next to someone who begins to laugh, even if you don't what's funny it is almost impossible not to laugh yourself. Laugh tracks have been used since 1950, when the radio comedy *The Hank McCune* show first used taped laugher to compensate for the lack of a live audience. Television executives learned that the same audience watching the same show would laugh much more readily when prompted by a laugh track. Just the simple act of hearing laughter makes you ready to laugh yourself. Too bad that some TV comedies are so bad the only laughter you hear at all is pre-recorded. Wouldn't it make sense to find the show the audience was watching when they taped the laughter and watch that show instead?

The Stevie Ray's Comedy Troupe has a performances piece called, "Laughing/Crying." It involves two performers improvising a sketch; one of the performers is the laugher and one is the crier. They deliver lines of dialogue as in any normal scene, except the laugher laughs at *everything* that is said, and the crier cries. When a director from outside the scene yells, "Switch," the laugher becomes the crier and vice versa. By the end of the scene the audience is on the floor laughing. The audience laughs simply because the laughter and tears of the actors draw them into the emotion of the scene. It is always amazing to see how similar the effect is of two such dissimilar emotions.

Professor Robert Provine of the University of Maryland Baltimore County, who conducted the ape study discussed in the introduction, conducted a different study of the contagious nature of laughter. He used an electronic laugh box to emit an eighteen-second span of laughter. When played for a group, almost half the listeners responded by laughing themselves, while ninety percent at least smiled upon hearing it. He played the laughter ten times in succession. Each time he played the laugh it was met with a smaller response from the listeners. By the end of the tenth laugh, most people reported that they actually found the laugh to be obnoxious. I guess we aren't particularly amused if someone else is having all the fun. And if there's is nothing to laugh *at*, we don't want to hear just plain laughter. Provine discovered that most people found repeated laughter more annoying than any other stimulus. For example, a person repeating a sentence ten times was not nearly annoying as hearing the laughter ten times. He reasoned that this is due to the fact that laughter is as often associated with ridicule as it is with joy.

Laughter has always been known to relieve stress and improve health, but only recently have physicians begun to recognize that laughter is more than just a physical luxury. Laughter is necessary for survival. When a person laughs, powerful chemicals called endorphins are released into the body. These endorphins cause the same reaction that morphine does when it is injected into the body, but with some profound differences. One difference is that endorphins can be hundreds or even thousands of times more powerful than the artificial drug, morphine. They have the same effect of blocking pain at the neural level and therefore give us a feeling of euphoria, but since endorphins are natural and more powerful, they are a more effective and healthy pain reliever. This extends to mental and emotional pain as well. When people meditate, exercise, or practice relaxation techniques, serum endorphin levels increase in the body and the person's mental state improves.

Another significant difference between morphine and endorphins is that endorphins don't just mask pain, they activate the immune system. It has long been said that laughter is the best medicine, and this old saying goes far beyond what you might expect. Most would think that laughter simply distracts one from the pain and discomfort of illness, making the illness easier to bear. In fact, laughter acts to combat the illness itself by doing what all physicians know is best, letting the body heal itself. A person with higher levels of endorphins also has elevated levels of T-cells, N-cells, and gamma globulins. These are necessary agents to fight bacteria and viruses. It is foolish of course to suggest that one should abandon modern medicine in favor of an afternoon of "Gilligan's Island" reruns, but patients around the world report a speedier recovery when humor is part of the treatment. We have known for some time that people who laugh and enjoy life are generally more healthy and live longer lives, now there is medical evidence to explain why.

The physical act of laughter does internally what a good masseuse or masseur does externally, massage what hurts. Trainers and physicians believe that exercise should include not only a good cardio vascular workout, but stretching and moving all the body parts. This massages the internal organs, increases blood flow, and loosens tissue. It is just as important to keep one's organs limber and supple as it is our arms and legs. Students of the ancient Japanese art of shiatsu, or acupressure, learn that the body has paths of internal energy called meridians. Our *Ki* (in China, *Chi*), or internal force, flows along these meridians. When two meridians cross, that point is called a *Tsuba*. When a blockage of energy occurs along a meridian or on a tsuba, sickness and poor health result. A shiatsu practitioner will press on the appropriate points to break the blockage and release the energy. A good bellylaugh shakes the body up and moves our insides around. It is the best internal massage if you can't afford a private rub-down everyday. Like all good exercise, the act of laughter creates physiological benefits one can feel immediately and chemical changes that create long-term benefits.

An interesting side note involves the neuropsychology of laughter and comes to us from a wonderful report published by Jonathon Miller, a doctor of medicine and a film, theatre, and opera director from Britain. In Dr. Miller's study, laughter has been classified as an "upper motor" involuntary function. It is involuntary because we can not choose when we laugh, and "upper motor" because it involves cognitive skill. Laughter, then, is unique from all other involuntary actions of the body because it starts in the cognitive center of the brain and moves down to affect lower functions of the body. Other involuntary acts such as pulse, breathing, blood vessel dilation, and sweating start from the "lower motor" neurons and subsequently affect the brain. We know that laughter is an upper-motor neuron function because patients affected with some types of brain disorders can still laugh, while those affected with other disorders can not.

In neurological wards of hospitals studies involving patients with Bell's Palsy show a marked difference in the ability to produce laughter than those affected by stroke. Bell's Palsy is an affliction that attacks the facial nerves, leaving the patient with paralysis on one half of the face. It is considered a lower-motor neuron defect because it affects the nerves in the face. These nerves are the lower part of the nervous system in that they are the last link in the chain between the brain and the muscle. In a stroke, a patient also suffers from partial paralysis, but it is considered an upper-motor neuron defect because the paralysis originates in the brain. The facial nerves are intact, but the brain does not send the necessary signals for them to stimulate muscle movement. The two disorders are alike in that if you were to ask either patient to smile, neither would be able to produce a smile on both sides of the face, indicating that they have no motor control on the paralyzed side. If you were to make a joke, however, the stroke patient will involuntarily smile on both sides of the face. The Bell's Palsy patient still only responds with a smile on one side of his face. This shows us that even though the act of laughter is indeed involuntary, it is a function of the higher centers of the brain. Almost all of our most important physical functions are involuntary. Breathing, heartbeat, response to pain, and hunger, are controlled for us so that our bodies can function efficiently and without conscious control. This also allows us to concentrate on matters of greater importance, like video games. If we didn't have an involuntary nervous system for these things, we would have to take up valuable brain space always thinking about our next meal. If you met some of my friends you would see that not everyone has evolved at the same rate. The act of smiling is not necessary for health, so it has remained a lower priority and left at the lower neural level. Proof that laughter is such a necessary part of survival is the fact that the brain has retained automatic control over its use.

Laughter is so important that it is not relegated to one hemisphere of the brain. In general, the left hemisphere of the brain is responsible for logic, reason, and analysis. The right hemisphere controls emotion, creativity, and feeling. One hemisphere of the brain in usually thought to control the motor skills of the opposite side of the body. This is why many people assume left-handed people are more creative, since they are governed by a dominant right hemisphere.

Studies have shown that there is no one part of the brain that is responsible for understanding humor. The right side of the brain, being emotive, generally controls a person's ability to comprehend and interpret punchlines of jokes. Much of the humor in comedy is delivered through attitude, so a strong sense of feeling is important. Comprehension certainly affects a person's ability to laugh, but patients who have suffered damage to the left hemisphere also suffer the inability to distinguish correct (funny) or incorrect punchlines in sample jokes. Patients with right-brain damage show an inability to recognize humor, either when performed in a sketch or on the written page. This is due in part to their inability to distinguish appropriate or inappropriate social behavior. Laughter appears to be a product of both sides of our brain working together. One side must comprehend meaning, and the other must feel the humor.

Chapter 10
THE CONDITIONS OF LAUGHTER

A very delicate balance must be maintained in order for a person to laugh. In any particular situation, certain conditions must be present for a person to laugh, the omission of any one will result in no laughter. We are a social animal and therefore subject to social restrictions. These restrictions often dictate whether a moment is appropriate to laugh. The specific conditions also work together to meet the need of a person to feel a part of the joke. The fact that the mind likes to make interesting connections to discover humor also dictates what conditions are necessary for a joke to be funny. And, as I discussed earlier, the need for the listener not to feel controlled or pushed into laughter will also come into play. The Laws of Laughter are the conditions that must be in place for laughter to occur. The skillful practitioner takes advantage of these conditions to create humor. There are however, subtle and often unconscious things a person can do that destroy these conditions. Those who aspire to be funny, whether on stage or in everyday life, should take special care to preserve these elements. These three conditions are the foundation of laughter and work in harmony: *A feeling of Detachment, A Light-Hearted Atmosphere,* and *Permission to Laugh.*

A Feeling of Detachment

In order to laugh you must feel a distance or lack of concern for the person you are laughing at. If your friend slipped on an icy sidewalk, you are more likely to laugh only if you know your friend isn't really hurt. If your grandmother slipped, there is a strong chance she could get hurt. In that case only an insensitive lout would laugh (at least, that's what she called me). A common phrase to explain laughter is, *"Comedy is tragedy that happens to someone else."* This is true as long as the tragedy involves loss of dignity, not loss of limb.

The condition of detachment is a major issue because it dictates the very subject matter a comedian selects. All humor must have a target, our laughter must be pointed at someone or something. In order to achieve true detachment however, we must know that the target is someone who can defend himself, someone incapable of real harm from the laughter. Politicians and leaders of society are timeless targets of jokes. Who better to attack than the most powerful people we know? Every society and every culture has jokes about their leaders. Humor, in that respect, is truly universal. Interesting too, that it rarely matters what a persons political views are when it comes to laughing at the leader. If you are a democrat and a republican made derogatory remarks about the democratic president, you would argue. No matter what political party occupies the oval office, *everyone* laughs at jokes about the president. With late night TV hosts and comedians in night clubs, we've come to expect president jokes to be a part of the act.

Joking about leaders starts as soon as we are able to comprehend humor. Most movies made for children use the same character devices; smart and capable children fooling stupid adults. Children's lives are under constant control by parents, teachers, and older siblings. Humor for youngsters must give them the same feeling of power that we adults demand. The only targets they have are us. Kind of makes you afraid to go to sleep, doesn't it?

The tricky thing about detachment is that it can't go too far. If we are so detached from a subject that we don't car at all about it, we would find the material too irrelevant to laugh about. So a good comedic performer must choose subject matter that is relevant to our lives, but not too close to hurt. That is why jokes are rarely pointed at defenseless segments of society; the mentally handicapped, the poor, the homeless. It is too difficult to feel detached to these subjects, so laughter at their expense is unlikely. The "politically correct" movement also greatly influenced what is considered appropriate targets of humor.

The acceptability of a target group changes constantly, which keeps comedians on their toes. For decades people told jokes about women–women drivers, mothers-in-law, women in the workplace–but when society deemed such jokes as hurtful to women, the target shifted (to blondes). The next big target was homosexuality. People react much the same as children when faced with a person or lifestyle that is foreign to them, they exert their control and power by ridiculing the group. Our need to bond with those familiar to us results in laughter pointed at anyone outside our circle. Once we become familiar with the new group, we feel less threatened and the jokes fade. With homosexuals the transformation to being an unacceptable target was two-fold. As the gay population gained more social and political power, more homosexuals "came out," no longer hiding their lifestyle. This meant that more and more "straight" people would meet and get to know gays and discover they were no different than themselves. Many straights discovered that they were acquainted with gays all along and just didn't know it. This made the gay population an *unnecessary* target. And, as with jokes about women, it was made clear that humor pointed at homosexuals was hurtful, making gays an *unacceptable* target.

Once a population changes from acceptable to unacceptable on the comedy scale, jokes against them actually have the opposite effect as before. As segments of the population lose their position as comedy targets, those who continue to ridicule them with cruel jokes are looked upon as backwards, uneducated, hateful, or ignorant. The sharp edge of comedy can swing in many directions, so one must be ever careful of their target of humor.

Light-hearted Atmosphere

Have you ever noticed that when you attend a comedy performance, if everyone is laughing you are more likely to laugh, even if the performance is not stellar? If everyone at a social gathering in is a good mood, simple conversation that would otherwise be considered dull becomes funny. As we learned from the laugh-track studies done for television, laughter generate laughter. For a person to laugh, a mood must *pre-exist* in the room that puts people in the mood to laugh. Once the mood is in place, laughter is not only easier, it almost creates itself. If an entire audience is laughing at a pratfall in a show, you will most likely laugh even if you didn't find it particularly funny. I've had friends laugh their heads off and still say on the way home, "I didn't think that guy was all that funny."

Most people easily recognize this condition. When out with friends they take advantage of the mood and joke the night away. We have so much fun with our buddies that we don't want the night to stop. As soon as one funny story ends, someone has to jump in with another or the room feels empty. There are those, however, who notice a somber room and try to *force* a light-hearted atmosphere. It's these idiots who think they can lighten up a room by pointing out the fact that everyone is depressed, "Hey! Who died? Come on you guys, it's a party! Woooo Woooooooooooooo!" Boy. Now I'm in the mood. These are the oafs I would like to sentence to life in the bedpan unit of a nursing home.

A group of people, whether an audience at a club or a party gathering, most easily develops a light-hearted mood when they are simply *relaxed*. The leader of the group, or the comedian on stage, can best establish a relaxed state of mind by displaying confidence. When we see a comedic attitude from someone who is truly confident we can relax because we know someone is in control. We trust that person to lead us into fun.

Mood. It's why operators of rides at amusement parks are trained to say exactly the right thing. To put us in the mood for a good ride. Imagine if you got on a rollercoaster and some teenage slouch said, *"Okay, sit there and try not to throw up on anyone when you hit the big loop. Have fun and I'll be here when you get back, still earning minimum wage."* The line for that ride would be pretty short. The Disney Corporation knows why people go to their theme parks, to laugh and have a day of fantasy. Every employee from the Spinning Teacup ride operator to the janitor is given a script that must be followed to the letter. The language of the script is designed for one purpose, to keep us in a light-hearted mood.

"Oooo. Look around the corner. I'm not sure we're safe in these waters. There could be pirates! Oh no, here comes one now! Let's see if this boat can get us out of here. Watch out you don't get sprayed by the fat hippo!"

If you were walking down the sidewalk and someone sprayed you with a hose, you would probably punch him in the nose. Here you are at Disneyland getting soaked by a fiberglass hippopotamus and you laugh your head off. The tightly scripted delivery of the operator maintains the exact mood the theme park needs to generate laughter. And Disney knows what good comedians know, the person at the helm better show confidence, or the group isn't going to feel comfortable enough to laugh.

Comedians playing in a night club and actors performing on a stage have the luxury of playing to an audience that is already predisposed to laugh. They are coming to the theatre with the expectation of laughter, so they are already in a light-hearted mood. The performer can not rest on this assumption though, because a bad comedian can easily ruin a light-hearted mood. The quickest way to destroy an audiences great mood is to show *nervousness*. The audience is there to laugh and they know that the only way they're going to get it is if the performer leads them there. If the comedian shows discomfort, the audience can not sit back and relax. Instead they feel empathy for the struggling comedian. Empathy turns to nervousness on his behalf. Nervousness finally develops into anxiety. The light-hearted atmosphere has transformed into the same mood parents have while watching their son or daughter in a grade school play. A person who would laugh at a comedian who is nervous and not performing well is a clod who enjoys others failure. Contrary to popular belief, you don't actually see many of those people in a comedy club. Like I said before, the only reason they're at the club is to have fun, and the comedian bombing isn't getting them there. So all a good comedian has to do is, no matter what, *never let them see you sweat.*

Permission to Laugh

Ever laugh at a funeral? While passing a school bus crash? After your mother drops the turkey at Thanksgiving dinner? Don't do the last one. I saw my mom's face turn colors they don't even have in a jumbo box of crayola crayons. You could be in a great mood yourself while passing a car accident, you could be completely detached from the other drivers, they could be jumping around in very funny ways, but in that particular situation *you don't have permission to laugh.*

It is the permission to laugh that allows us to temporarily drop concerns of etiquette and courtesy and laugh at someone else's misfortune. We know that we can laugh at the person who just had a bucket of water drop on her head if her attitude shows us that it's okay. We have to get permission from either the person who is the target of humor, or from the group we are with. If everyone starts laughing, we know it's safe. If one person's laughing and the rest of the crowd is glaring at him, you know to keep your mouth shut.

The lack of permission is what keeps us from laughing at things that would ordinarily have us on the floor. I remember my father yelling at me as a young boy (I can't believe he was so unreasonable about one little brush fire in the back yard). Right in the middle of his tirade, he farted. Now, I'm like any red-blooded young American male, farts are the essence of comedy. As any boy would do, I giggled. It was then that I learned the true meaning of *permission to laugh*, because I didn't have it. I also didn't have feeling below the waist for three days.

Chapter 11
THE LAWS OF LAUGHTER

Once all the conditions have been met for laughter to be both possible and appropriate, certain mental states must exist in the audience for laughter to be produced. Laughter can be separated into two main areas: *comedic laughter*, and *instinctive laughter*. Comedic laughter is a response to a situation, whether theatric or social. It can occur in an arena, such as a theatre or comedy club, or in everyday situations. It is not necessarily planned, nor does the person laughing or the person inciting the laugh always realize that laughter will be the result. There are four main sources of comedic laughter:

- *Laughter of the Unexpected*
- *Laughter of Recognition*
- *Laughter of Superiority*
- *Laughter of Delight.*

In all forms of comedy, all of these conditions must be present for laughter to occur. They work in harmony to create humor. If you remove one, a necessary element is missing, a key emotion is absent that produces a laugh.

Laughter of the Unexpected

"I'll bet you didn't see that coming!"

Think back to the last time someone told you a joke or story that you had already heard before. Or, worse yet, she told a new joke so badly that you could guess the ending before she reached it. There was no way you could really laugh when she "gave away the ending." At most, you can give an obligatory chuckle so you don't lose a friend, or so she will do the same when you deliver a bomb yourself. Laughter doesn't occur unless there is a surprise, an unexpected twist in the story, joke, or situation. Surprise is crucial to good comedy. Without it you simply have a pleasant story. Surprise is important for all levels of comedy.

An infant is surprised at physical humor, even though the parent repeats the peek-a-boo motion many times. The infant is much like a dog who is fooled repeatedly by the same trick of hiding a bone behind your back. Neither has the intellectual capability to discern and anticipate a pattern. As you grow older your ability to anticipate the unexpected sharpens and the level of comedy must be higher in order to be enjoyable. The humor of physical comedy plays upon a person's natural tendency to develop expectations based on experience. When a person is walking down the street we expect the pattern to continue until he reaches to bus stop. When the person trips, our natural expectations aren't met, we are caught off-guard, and we laugh.

As you cross from low comedy to high, where the humor is based on ideas, the surprise is based on unexpected thoughts instead of visuals. The ideas presented in satire are so outrageous that they surprise us into laughter. Everyday we hear people insult the boss, complain about congress, and lament about relationships, but we do not expect people to actually imitate them so that every detail of their actions are held up to ridicule. It is one thing to sit with a group of your friends around the bar and say, "Doesn't the president suck?" "Yeah, how did he ever get elected anyway?" It is quite another for someone to stand up, assume the posture and mannerisms of Nixon and say, "I am not a crook," in a perfect deep-voiced copy of the former president. Complaints are expected; they are part of the routine. To break out of the routine and take the complaints one step further creates a surprise and laughter.

Laughter of the unexpected is why modern comedy is such a difficult art form to perfect. As audiences grow more and more familiar with comedy performance, it becomes increasingly more difficult to surprise them. Many comedians resort to the easy laugh of breaking a taboo, such as swearing on stage or using shocking or distasteful subject matter. This would explain why comedy seems to grow more shocking every year. As audiences grow more accustomed to risqué material, these comedians feel they must step outside normal boundaries to find good material.

Old style comedians who had to follow much stricter censorship laws, found laughs in clever wordplay. See where the surprise hits in Allen Sherman's parody, sung to the tune of "Greensleeves." It helps to know a bit about Jewish culture.

In Sherwood Forest there dwelt a knight
who was known as the righteous Sir Green...baum.
And many dragons had felt the might
of the smite of the righteous Sir Greenbaum.
I chanced upon him one morn,
when he'd recently rescued a maiden fair.
"Why, why art thou so forlorn?
Sir Greenbaum, is thy heart heavy laden?"
Said he, "For sooth, 'tis a sorry plight
that engendered my attitude blueish."
Said he, "I don't want to be a knight.
That's no job for a boy who is Jewish."
"All day with the mighty sword, and the mighty steed, and the mighty lance.
All day with that heavy shield, and a pair of aluminum pants.
All day with the slaying, and slewing, and smiting and smoting like Robin Hood.
Oh, would'st I could kick the habit, and give up smoting for good."
And so he said to the other knights,
"You may have my possessions and my goods.
For I am moving to Shaker Heights,
where I've got some connections in dry goods."
"Farewell to the Dragon's Paw,

136

and the other swashbuckling games and sports.
I'll work for my father-in-law,
when I marry miss Guenevere Schwartz."
             "Sir Greenbaum's Madrigal"
             Allen Sherman
             My Son, the Folk Singer

Laughter of the unexpected taps into a base instinct of man. There is no pre-thought or intellectual connection made on the part of the listener. Because laughter of the unexpected takes listeners completely by surprise, it can even cause people to laugh even if they don't want to. How many times have you been watching a comedian you found distasteful and you ended up laughing anyway? You disliked the performer so much you *decided* not to laugh, but the comedian said something so unexpected you laughed in spite of yourself.

What destroys the unexpected is poor delivery or a meandering plot line. Always remember this simple fact, *there is no way for you to speak faster than the listener can think.* Since the brain can think at such a high speed, while the audience is listening to a story they are also guessing where the story is leading and what the ending might be. This goes along with the function of the brain that was discussed earlier, that of filling in the blanks. It is easy to surprise people with a funny ending to a story if there is no foretelling that the ending will be funny. People tend to follow patterns and if a story is being told with a serious attitude the listener will assume that seriousness will continue. If the story has a goofy ending the surprise has been set up effectively and the listener will laugh.

If the setting is already comedic, such as performing an act in a comedy club, the listener expects that the end of every story or routine will be funny. In both the somber and comedic situation the audience will automatically think ahead, but in the comedic setting the audience will be guessing the punch line. If the comedian takes too long to get to the end of the story, the audience is there waiting, and with quite a few possible funny endings figured out already. A good performer knows to keep the story moving so as not to give the audience a chance to beat him to the punchline.

Laughter of Recognition

"Someday we'll look back on this and laugh."

It has often been said, "There's nothing new in comedy." Some believe that no new ideas have been presented since the caveman ancestor of Stan Laurel stubbed his toe and scratched the top of his head while the rest of the tribe howled with laughter. If you watch any kind of comedy program—stand-up, sit-com, play, or sketch revue—you would undoubtedly see the same themes recycled over and over again. Is nothing new in comedy? Why are we laughing if we've seen the joke, or a version of it, a hundred times before? This is where the laughter of recognition applies. Laughter of recognition involves people seeing a situation or person on stage and recognizing it from real life. The memory of their own actions and the occasion to see them played out in front of them causes laughter. If enough time has lapsed since our own trip to the dentist, we can laugh at a comedian reenacting the whole experience. *Comedy is tragedy plus time.* If not enough time has passed, we'll sit sullenly as everyone else has a good time. *We'll look back on this someday and laugh.*

Our ability to laugh at ourselves is thought to be a release of tension, an emotional safety-valve. If we didn't laugh at our problems, the stress would build up to the point where we would be in a constant state of agitation. Laughing at ourselves helps take a bad memory and lessen the pain. Many of the situations used for laughter of recognition are instances of embarrassment or misfortune. This allows us as an audience to review an unhappy memory in a happy environment.

Lenny Bruce, in his routine "The Phone Company," uses our collective fear of dealing with institutions of authority to generate laughter out of a tense situation.

I really don't dig the phone company anyway. It's a monopoly. If you get too hot with the phone company you'll end up with a Dixie Cup and a thread. Where you gonna go besides them? Now, I'm 33 now. When I was about 19 or 20 I was really hot with the phone company. But I used to like, make a long distance call in a dark gas station.

"This is the long distance operator. That'll be three dollars and seventy cents for overtime."

"Lots o' luck!"

"What?"

"Forget the money, you're not getting it."

"Well I don't understand...."

"It's not too hard to understand, you're not getting the money, that's all. You don't need it anyway, right? Don't be a company girl. Forget it, you're not getting it."

"Well I don't understand...."

"Well you're not getting it."

"I'm going to give you the supervisor.

"I can't wait." (sarcastically)

"This is the supervisor."

"Ahh you nitwit."

"Could we have your name, sir?"

"Yes, it's Mort Sahl."

Poor Mort gets phone calls every...Tijuana is the greatest place in the world to make phone calls.

"Hello, de Telefonices de Tijuana."

"I want to call Beverly Hills. I want Crestview 45506."

"Okay, that's going to be seven dollars and fifty cents."

"What's the matter?"

"I've only got four dollars."

"Put it in."

Yeah, you could add some Chicklets, a sweater....

Lenny Bruce

The Best of Lenny Bruce

It is amazing to see a skillful comedian describe situations that seem to be right out of our own lives, accurate down to the smallest detail. Groups of people who live together in a relatively closed society experience the same things in the same progression while growing up. Sociologists have written books describing common rituals of dating, marriage, employment, and leisure activities. People who read these descriptions can't believe how accurate the details can be. Talk shows find that, no matter how tragic a story the guest tells, there are hundreds of audience members who relate to the exact some story.

Comedians and writers rely on this phenomenon to create laughter of recognition. They examine the moments from their own lives that affected them strongly and perform them on stage. The audience is shocked at how the comedians life mirrors their own. In my own experience as a comedian, I have found that I can tell stories from my life with absolutely no embellishment and receive many laughs. Audience members have often told me that they have done the exact same things in their lives. Thus, laughter of recognition offers people an opportunity to say, through laughter, "See, we are all the same. I'm not the only jerk in the crowd." Our need to bond as a community as served by a common source of humor.

Laughter of recognition also takes advantage of our own feelings of insecurity. People have a way of making much more out of their own shortcomings than those of their friends; we all stumble through life feeling like we are singularly the biggest idiot in the world. Laughter of recognition eases these feelings of inadequacy, or at least spreads them around evenly. When someone tells a story of a big mix-up in their life and we have encountered the same problem, we experience a sense of

141

euphoria that we are not as big a loser as we thought. Self-help groups thrive on the singular principle that to talk to a group of people who have the same problem as you is therapeutic. Even if no real analysis of your problem is performed, being with a group who has suffered through your situation feels good. Laughter performs the same function for society as a whole.

A need for common ground is why there are certain comedy themes that recur throughout the ages. People only encounter a number of experiences that are common to all. We all get up every day, try to earn a living, deal with relationships, want to buy cool toys, have sex, eat, drive, wait in airports, shower, pee, and try to get a good nights sleep. The larger the audience, the more general the topic needs to be in order to ensure recognition. Comedians performing on national TV programs have millions of people to connect with. People don't care that there are no big new ideas, as long as the ideas that are used have some relationship with their lives.

Luckily for comedians, the audience allows some leeway in the connection to their common experience. Not every situation in a comedy story has to have been lived by the audience as long as the audience can understand and put themselves in the comedians shoes. I tell a story in my act about the first time I ever went water-skiing and what a disaster it was. I learned never to take your brothers when learning a life-threatening activity. They don't care about safety, they want *entertainment value.* My inexperience at water-skiing, Dick's 200 horsepower speed boat, and Mike's eye for finding every stump and rock in the lake made for an obstacle course training session the marines would be proud of. Of every audience member who has heard the routine and laughed, only half have every water-skied themselves. They have, however, seen water-skiing on TV and have been in situations where they were not physically up to a challenge. It is not necessary that everyone has done exactly what you are describing, as long as they can imagine themselves in the situation and empathize with your plight, laughter of recognition is yours.

Laughter of Superiority

Freedom produces jokes, and jokes produce freedom
Jean Paul Richter, 1804

What a sap, what a maroon, what a ta-ra-ra-goon-dee-ay
Buggs Bunny

Introduced earlier was the theory that the laughter of modern man is simply an evolution of the victory cry of an ape. When apes beat an opponent, they stand over the fallen victim, and let out a yell to express delight, victory, and to announce to the rest of the apes, "Here stands a strong dude. Best keep your distance." This may not be the most flattering picture of modern man, but it is an accurate description of the true source of laughter. Think about it. Was there ever a time in your life that you laughed if there wasn't someone who was the brunt of the joke? The answer is of course, no. In every event that includes laughter, someone has to be the target of the humor.

Every joke is either pointed at the listener, the teller, or a third party not in the room. In any case, someone has been made the fool.

Our own feelings of inadequacy constantly make us look for ways to cut others down, to gently even the playing field. It was Plato who first said that laughter is the result of our feelings of superiority over another person who is involved in an unfortunate situation. We laugh because we are not in the same predicament, and are too wise to allow ourselves to act so stupidly.

Good performers know how to use our need for superiority to their advantage. In fact, most comedians can be divided into those who pick on the audience, and those who pick on themselves. Self-deprecating humor assures that the audience will always be on your side, against yourself. George Burns and Gracie Allen relied on Gracie's character to be naive and dim-witted. In fact, we laughed <u>at</u> her even when she showed herself to be wiser than she let on. See how she slips a compliment for herself in a conversation about her first trip to the ballet.

Gracie: Oh gee, everybody was there. Did you notice Bob Tayler and Barbara Stanwyck sitting in front of us?

George: Yeah, that Barbara Stanwyck certainly is gorgeous.

Gracie: I'll say. Those actors really marry beautiful women, don't you George?

Laughter is a very effective tool for reinforcing our superiority because it is both direct and immediate. There is never any doubt as to who is being made fun of in a joke, and the resulting laughter joins the whole crowd together, creating a group bond that lifts everyone's self-image. It's as if we say, "No matter how stupid I am, at least I'm not as bad as that guy, and everyone here agrees with me or they wouldn't be laughing too." Our feelings of superiority are never as strong as when we have verbal support from our friends. Laughter is the most visible, immediate, and unmistakable means of support there is. If I'm sitting with a group of friends at a bar and make a derogatory joke against another table of people, a quick look at who's laughing will instantly tell me who supports me. Sometimes people will laugh with a comrade to show support, even if what is said isn't particularly funny.

Laughter of superiority is an instant way to solidify and distinguish groups. Take, for instance, the ethnic or regional joke. Ethnic jokes were popular at various times throughout history as a result of certain groups' lack of social power. These targets were easy because they did not have the status necessary to fight back, either verbally or socially. As opposed to today, the lack of "politically correct" rules allowed jokes directed at defenseless targets to flourish. Ethnic jokes still exist today, but they do not enjoy the widespread support they received decades ago.

Laughter of superiority is often used by those in power to reassert their position. This is because those at the top of the hill are the ones who have the most to lose if they fall.

Powerful people live in fear of losing what they have. If an ethnic group moved into an area and threatened the status quo, jokes were developed to rally the troops and point out "them" from "us." When that ethnic group gained enough power to be of the same class as the "us", jokes were shifted to a different, less powerful group. Historically derogatory humor in America has shifted from the Jews, to the Irish, to the Polish, to blacks, to women, to Middle Easterners (during the Iran Crises and the Gulf War), to blonde women, to homosexuals, and back around the circle. Some people get stuck on one group and make jokes about them even after their time has passed. Comedians have a term for these joke tellers...boring.

A (insert race, religion, or gender) *walked into a hardware store and said to the owner, "You sold me a chainsaw and said it would cut five cords of wood a day. This one only cuts three cords." The owner said, "Maybe you need a bigger saw, here try this one." The next day the* (insert) *returned and said, "This one only cuts two cords." The owner said, "Let's see what's wrong with it." He started up the chainsaw and the* (insert) *said, "What's that noise?"*

Jokes based on race, gender, or other social classification are meant not only to demean that class, but in effect "keep them in their place." As our society became more sensitive to the plight of the socially oppressed, the ethnic joke was largely removed from the comedy arsenal. As would be expected, a reversal occurred. As minority groups gained social power, the

146

use of ethnic joke against whites became popular. In an atmosphere of banding together, jokes that placed whites in the role of the fool gained popularity. Major comedy productions like "Def Comedy Jam," "Evening at the Apollo," and "Phat Comedy Jam," as well as in comedy clubs across the country, the opening line, "You white folks do some strange things...." became common. In fact, while visiting a comedy club in my home state of Minnesota, the host (a black gentleman performing for a largely black audience) spent at least ten minutes introducing the next comedian as one of only three white men in the entire show. Laughter of superiority is used to gain footholds in society and garner support from one's own group.

A somewhat harmless replacement for the ethnic joke has always been the regional joke. An "us versus them" mentality has existed ever since people started forming tribes. People striving for a common goal will even poke fun at each other if they are from different geographic regions. Each state in America has its rival state, and jokes against residents of that state are never-ending. Minnesota makes joke against Iowa, California against Nevada, and North Dakota against South Dakota (there's a difference?). In each case the target is a neighbor, and that neighbor is perceived as unequal to the home state. The butt of the joke being a neighbor state ensures that there is enough familiarity to give power to the joke. Much like a comedian would not expect the audience to laugh at the expense of a person they did not know, North Carolina would not make jokes about Utah.   Instead they would joke about a neighbor, Tennessee.

A set of criteria exists for one state to joke about another. In most cases the "lesser" state has an economy that relies more on agriculture and blue collar jobs. It also does not have the standard of living or level of education the "good" state possesses. Minnesota regards Iowa as a "farm state" filled with "dumb farm people."   California sees Nevada as a California wanna-be state, trying vainly to imitate their glitz and glamour. North and South Dakota—who knows? If a state is surrounded by states that are similar in these respects, then all the neighboring states are targets.   I have performed in comedy shows and asked where certain audience members were from. A heckling laughter arose in the audience whether the person said any neighboring state of Minnesota; Iowa, Wisconsin, North Dakota, or South Dakota. The demeaning attitude is so entrenched that I would rarely have to say anything funny about the neighboring state; people would start laughing before a joke was ever told.   You see why no one ever leaves Minnesota— we're too afraid of what our friends would say about us after we were gone.

Do you know why the Grand Canyon exists?
A Dutchman lost a dime.

Many ethnic or regional jokes take advantage of stereotypes by exaggerating them for the sake of humor.

Jerry Stiller and Anne Meara formed the comedy duo, *Stiller and Meara*, reminiscent of Nichols and May. Their sketch, *Hershey Horowitz-Mary Elizabeth Doyle, Wedding Plans*, shows an interesting twist of the ethnic/regional joke. The humor comes from hearing two lovers declare their passion for each other amid the constant misunderstanding of their respective Irish and Jewish backgrounds. The routine starts on an affectionate note, but the ethnic and religious confusion continually creates anxiety.

Hershey: I love you Mary Elizabeth Doyle.
Mary: Oooo I love you Hershey Horowitz.
Will you marry me?
Yeah, I will. I will.
It'll never work. My father's a Jewish bagel baker. Your father's an Irish cop.
What difference?
What do you mean, what difference? It's like a hot pastrami on...on white bread.
It doesn't matter. We love each other. Look, Hershey, it'll work out. The families will go crazy for each other.
They'll go crazy, that's what they'll do.
Oh come on. I'll grab your mother, I'll hug her, I'll kiss her. I'll say, "Mrs. Horowitz, you're terrific. I hear you make the best meshugganah-ball   soup in the world."
Matzah-Ball Soup! Yes, yes, yes. That's it, that's it, you tell her that.

And I'll say, "Gee, you know where we're going? Your son and I are going to go to Israel on our honeymoon. We're going to live on a Knish for a couple of weeks."

On a <u>Kibbutz</u>! Beautiful, beautiful.

After this, they have trouble deciding the wedding date

Springtime. How about March?

March is no good you're running right into Ash Wednesday, Lent, and Easter.

Oh, that's no good.

How about April or May.

Now you got Pesach, Purim, and Shavuos.

Honey, it doesn't matter.

It doesn't matter! The important thing is that we love each other, right?

Then they have to decide about the band for the reception.

I know just who I want.

Who?

Lenny Hershwitz and the Orchestra.

Who's that? I never heard of them.

He plays great Kazotsky's, Russian Chairs, Frelichs.

What's that? The one with the "huch?"

You mean "Frelich."

Yeah, what is that?

You know, Frelich. (Sings Hebrew melody) *Dai dai dai dai...*

It's very catchy. Honey, I was hoping to get my cousin to play for us.

Your cousin?

Yeah, Tommy Tewey and his Donny Gold Five. They are great!

Do they play the Kazotsky?

Well, they play the Knights of Columbus.

Hey wait a minute, we'll have alternating orchestras.

Great!

And in between we'll have Pepe Melito and the Rhumbas.

Great. Then we don't offend nobody.

> Jerry Stiller and Anne Meara
> Ed Sullivan Presents:
> The Last Two People in the World

Regional joke conditions exist for nations as well as states. The Polish joke of the 60s and the Irish joke before that demonstrate that whenever a class of people immigrate to a new country, they are the target of jokes. These jokes invariably follow the same theme, that the new class of people are stupid and inept. Often the jokes are a result of the insecurity felt by the natives of the new country. More immigrants mean more competition for jobs, the introduction of strange lifestyles, and a questioning of the lifestyle of the host country. In fact, it is not necessary to immigrate to a country to become the butt of jokes, as long as the nation that is the object of the joke is seen as less developed, lower class, or uneducated. Just like our states, nations have their favorite targets. Britain jokes about the Irish, France about the Swiss, Dutch about the Belgians, Sweden about the Finns, and Brazil about the Portuguese. In every case, the target of the joke is a nation that is more reliant upon agriculture for its industry, and therefore a less desirable place to live.

Regional attacks are so pervasive that I have met people who were being transferred to Iowa with their job after living in Minnesota all their lives. These people were horrified at the prospect of living in the "stupid state," when in fact, there is no appreciable difference between the two. I often wonder how long after moving to Iowa these same people were making Minnesota jokes. I wouldn't know, because I refuse to live there!

Laughter of Delight

Remember the last big sporting event you saw? You had a lot riding on that game: school pride, money, your son or daughter was on the team. Toward the end of the game things were not going well; those big bullies on the other team were cheating and your team was behind with no hope in sight. Just as it seemed the game was lost, your team burst out and, in the last few seconds of the game, took the lead and won. You threw your hands in the air, jumped up and down, and *laughed*. Why were you laughing? Nothing was really funny. No one fell down, the referee didn't make any goofy gestures, there certainly wasn't anything satiric. There was no act or situation that would seem to cause laughter.

Laughter of delight is its own source and cause of laughter. It is a direct physical reaction to a mental state. Our emotions build up so much that unless some outlet is provided, we will mentally explode. Some would look at the above situation and think that the laughter is caused by a feeling of superiority over the opposing team, but that is not entirely accurate. Watch an audience viewing a performance of gymnastics, or a skilled juggler. Occasionally the audience will let loose a laugh, yet there is no one to whom they feel superior, especially since the performers are accomplishing feats of skill that far surpass their own. Humans are a visually stimulated animal, and viewing feats of skill produces positive emotions. The emotions continue to build up, especially if the performer is wise enough to create a climax for the act by saving the most impressive and flashy feat for last. Laughter becomes a release, an extension of the physical condition of the body. As we become excited our blood pressure increases, our pulse and breathing quicken, our muscles tense, chemicals are released into the bloodstream that put our bodies into the classic "flight or fight" condition. As happy as the situation is, the physical manifestation of the emotion is actually creating a negative build-up of tension in the body. To sustain this physical condition for any length of time is harmful, and the unconscious mind that monitors our physical state must act in order to relieve the pressure. The next thing you know, you're laughing. This is no different than the person who cries at a sad movie. Sometimes while watching a sad scene in a play or movie, you begin to cry even though you physically try to prevent it. The body is creating a physical release for the build-up of tension. The brain uses laughter to protect the body, and the reaction is gauged to be socially acceptable—laughter at a fun event, tears at a sad one.

The movie *The Ref* starred comedian-turned-actor Dennis Leary as a thief. In the story Leary must hold a dysfunctional family hostage until he can escape town undetected by the police. Lloyd and Caroline, the husband and wife, are at a difficult point in their marriage. They argue constantly, their son is a delinquent, and their in-laws are a meddling bunch of spiteful, whining brats. Lloyd's mother, sister, and her husband and two children are at the house to celebrate Christmas Eve. Even though Lloyd and Caroline can't stand each other and argue constantly, we begin to feel empathy for them, partly because as objective audience members we can see that they each are equally to blame for their problems, and also because they each have good qualities that the other ignores. As the movie progresses we learn that many of their problems are caused by his mother and sister, and her family. Toward the end of the movie, in order to escape, Leary's character, Gus, ties and gags all the in-laws. By this point in the movie Lloyd and Caroline have begun to see that their marital problems are the result of his family. After Gus escapes and they are freed, they are left in the house with a tied-up family. They have discovered that they do love each other and have finally told off the rest of the family. As they kiss, Lloyd asks, "So, do you think we should go untie everybody?" Caroline responds, "No. We should unwrap them in the morning. It'll be more festive."

The laughter Caroline's response causes comes at a crucial point in the movie. We have developed a liking for Lloyd and Caroline. We want them to stay together and work out their problems, but throughout the movie there is a threat of divorce.

154

We also develop a strong dislike for the in-laws. They forever run on at the mouth about Lloyd and Caroline's shortcomings. We wish they would simply shut up. When Gus gags them, we get our wish. When Caroline and Lloyd decide to leave them tied up and openly insult them, we get our second wish. Even though the line about leaving them tied up is not particularly funny, we laugh because it is the point of the story that gives us the greatest relief. The line is somewhat unexpected, and gives us a feeling of superiority over the in-laws. We have recognition of the situation (from disagreements with our own families), and we laugh out of delight. Laughter of delight because of a release of tension and a wish to support their decision.

Laughter of delight provides the same benefit as laughter of recognition, the solidifying of a group. When groups of people are satisfied with the result of an event—a favorite team winning, a skilled performer executing a difficult technique, or the happy conclusion to a story—we not only reward the performers with laughter, we reinforce our unity as a group.

Instinctive Laughter

Instinctive laughter is separate from comedic laughter because it comes from a different part of the mind. There are so many benefits to laughter that the brain has created many different situations in which it is a response. Sometimes laughter is not so much a delightful luxury as it is a defense mechanism. Although all laughter is partly instinctive, since there isn't a lot of time for the mind to ponder whether or not to laugh at a given situation, for the purposes of distinction I say that *instinctive laughter* is that which is a reaction, not a response. As opposed to comedic laughter, instinctive laughter is a reaction to stress and discomfort, not joy and celebration. There are two kinds of instinctive laughter: *subservient laughter* and *nervous laughter.*

Subservient Laughter

For some, instinctive laughter is an unconscious tactic, meant to gain approval from a superior. A young woman being interviewed for her first job might let out a quiet giggle. The interviewer will often feel obligated to respond by smiling, making light of the situation, or reassuring the woman in some way. In this situation, the laugh works to diffuse a tense situation. One could almost see a connection to the behavior of dogs in a pack, where the subservient dog will submissively roll on his or her back to gain support of the leader. Those who engage in subservient laughter are often not aware that the exchange is taking place, or that their laughter is creating a behavioral change in others.

Most people think they are just laughing because they are nervous. They are nervous, and part of their laughter could be characterized as nervous laughter. The difference is that subservient laughter is always done in a situation of hierarchy.

In every interaction between people, there is status involved. There is the obvious difference in status of boss/employee, parent/child, high priestess/sacrificial goat. In every relationship, there are status games. A boy who lets out a quiet laugh when he realizes that he forgot his girlfriend's birthday has just signified the loss of status. A new player on a team will laugh harder at a joke told by a veteran member than he would if his rookie roommate had told the same joke.

Most people don't play these games intentionally. They are merely reacting to a situation in which they have no power. Being in a powerless position is very threatening, and action must be taken to correct the situation. This is where the fight or flight reaction occurs. For some, the reaction is to fight, to bully their way to the top of the heap and regaining control. Others withdraw, preferring to blend in with the surroundings like a chameleon, hoping danger will pass by without noticing them. Others try to lighten the mood and create allies. Subservient laughter either accomplishes the task by winning over others with a light-hearted mood, or it fails miserably by aggravating those in power and making the laugher look weak and helpless.

In any case, laughter has protected its owner from attack, for even if a person of higher status is annoyed by laughter, rarely will he lash out at the laugher. This would make him look heartless and cruel.

Nervous Laughter

We have all been in tense situations where, for some reason, we begin to chuckle. Many people have been at a solemn occasion and been surprises by a person laughing. My favorite episode of the Mary Tyler Moore show is when she couldn't stop laughing during the funeral of her fellow television personality, Chuckles the Clown. The writers of the show created wonderful comic irony by developing an earlier scene in the show where Mary is angry at her co-workers, Lou, Murray, and Ted, for laughing at the manner in which Chuckles died (he was crushed by an elephant because he was dressed in a peanut costume). Lou tries to explain to Mary that sometimes people laugh as a way to deal with the uncomfortable issue of death. Mary won't hear of it and thinks the men are morbid and heartless. Later at the funeral, Mary's nervousness gets the best of her. The pastor starts listing off his favorite Chuckles the Clown characters, and Mary can not stifle her laughter. We not only laugh at the sight of Mary laughing, but at the thought of Mary's own admonishments backfiring on her. During the scene, Mary tries to bottle up her laughter while Lou, Murray, and Ted shoot her looks of disapproval. The dénouement of the scene is when the pastor can no longer ignore her laughter. He asks her to stand. While she is exposed to the entire congregation, humiliated, he tells her that it is okay to laugh. He tells the gathering that Chuckles spent his life making people laugh, and that to laugh now at his funeral would honor him and his work. It would be exactly what Chuckles would want. Upon hearing this Mary gathers herself up, takes a deep breath, and bursts out crying.

Many people are aware that their response to uncomfortable situations is laughter, and they are not always comfortable with that knowledge. People who say, "I always laugh when I get nervous. I hate it when I do that!" Laughter however, is a necessary function for the mental and physical health of a person. If we are in a situation that is uncomfortable, the mind sees this as a danger and will work to resolve the problem. For some people the solution is violence or aggression, for others it is an attempt to change the mood and remove the danger. To laugh during a tense situation is an attempt to change the atmosphere from a dangerous one to a calm one.

Nervous laughter works on physical as well as mental levels. The mental side of the laughter attempts to change the mood of a dangerous situation. The physical side is the body releasing tension by creating laughter. The shaking of the body, the expelling of air, increased blood flow, relaxing of the muscles, all cleanse the body of negative chemicals. The autonomic nervous system works to ensure the well-being of the body by engaging this system without the conscious control of the person. When the welfare of the body and mind are in jeopardy, actions like laughter can make a big difference.

Chapter 12
REWARD OR REPRIMAND

Against the assault of laughter, nothing can stand.
The Mysterious Stranger
Mark Twain

No matter how many *reasons* there are for laughter, there are two *results* of laughter: to reward for a wonderful performance, or to reprimand for being an idiot. When someone incites laughter in others it is usually by stepping outside of the rules of society. There are times when this taboo behavior is acceptable and even encouraged, such as in a comedy club or theatre where people go to specifically see someone break the rules. When the performer steps out of bounds we reward with laughter, much the same way as we rewarded the class clown by laughing at his or her antics in school, especially when the behavior was disruptive to the order of class. People have a way of wanting to see the underdog win. They want those in power brought down to size, and since laughter is the great equalizer, it is the quickest means to achieve that balance. We change very little from when we were children. The only thing that changes is the target, from the teacher to our boss or the president.

We laugh at the class clown because we are on his side. The clown and the student against Attila the Hun, the teacher. However, when someone who is not popular (the class nerd) takes a fall on the playground and lands in a puddle of water, we laugh not to reward the behavior, but to reprimand it. Through the laughter of superiority, we show people that they and their behavior are not acceptable, and that in order to be "in" with the crowd they will have to change. In this way, laughter has incredible power in the role of social control. Laughter is very effective at enforcing rules of behavior. Think back to the last time you felt really stupid in front of a group of friends or co-workers. It was probably not when a superior was yelling at you for making a mistake. Scolding usually inspires more anger than shame, which would make you more likely to resist changing your behavior in order to spite your boss. The most humiliating experience was to be laughed at by a group of peers. When you are the butt of a joke the situation is much different than if you are simply being criticized.

Criticism is usually a singular experience. Even if a group is present, it is the boss doing the yelling while everyone else sits silently staring at their coffee cups wishing they were in the lunchroom. If an entire group *laughs* at you because of your mistake, suddenly you have no allies, no one to turn to for support. And, since people are highly social animals (except for Howard Hughes), we will change our behavior to make sure we <u>never</u> get laughed at again. Whether you are being laughed *with* or *at* is a very important distinction in how laughter affects our behavior.

Chapter 13
COMEDY: HIGH AND LOW

There are two different classes of comedy: that which is merely a reaction to surprise or shock, and that which is a result of intellectual association. Low comedy is caused by shock, a surprise, a build up of expectations followed by a twist. High comedy also contains surprise and a build-up of expectation, but the humor of high comedy *makes a statement.* The statement can be simple critique, as in the comedy of sarcasm or verbal repartee, or it can be as complicated as a satirical send-up of our political system. The statement may be either about someone in particular or society in general. Very often the single individual is someone in a position of power, and therefor represents society in some way.

Both high and low comedy are immediate. Almost no form of comedy can exist if it is not, since too much thought can kill any joke. This makes high comedy much more difficult to produce. Burying an important message inside the joke is tricky, either the message is too subtle and is lost, or the joke is sacrificed because the message is too heavy. Many great comedic performers are adept at including both high and low comedy into their performance. Bill Cosby is well known for his detailed and hilarious descriptions of everyday events. In one routine, he describes going to the dentist:

Dentists tell you not to pick your teeth with any sharp metal object. Then you sit in their chair...and the first thing they grab is an iron hook. Now the dentist pulls out a needle. This is to deaden the pain. Now a regular doctor giving you a shot would go shpuck and that's it. Dentists don't do that they go shpuck (followed by motions of digging the needle around the mouth). *Then they want to talk to you.*

"Do you ever do any fishing?"

"Uh huh." (Said as if fingers are stuffed into mouth, followed by heavy painful breathing)

"Where do you usually go?"

"Wehu ai usai gu ou hou haw awiou uiouwe"

"Yes, I've been there many times myself."

Later in the routine

Now he drills some more, and you hear him make a mistake (sounds of drill ended by a wrenched sound). *And to cover it up they all say the same thing,*

"Okay, rinse."

"Ribinse? You ask me to ribinse. I don't habe a bottom libp, how can I   ribinse?"

"Give it a try."

...So you pick it up, pour it in, now you gotta spit into this miniature toilet bowl. You have no bottom lip so you let it all fall out. You say 'thank God for gravity'. Now you want to sit back, but you can't, because hanging from your bottom lip is a

long line, and you can't get it off your bottom lip. So you sit
back. Now you have a line from the bowl to your bottom lip.
The dentist looks at it and says, "Oh look, a rainbow!"

The humor of this piece is so diminished by merely seeing it
in print instead of hearing or watching Cosby perform live, but
it still shows that he is a master at using all levels of comedy in
his work. While performing the piece he assumes the posture
and motions of a patient undergoing dental work, *physical
comedy*. He unfolds an entire visit to the dentist piece by piece,
storyline. His first statement contains the deliberate use of the
words "iron hook," a wonderful exaggeration of a dentist's
pick, *language*, as well as the irony that dentists tell you not to
pick your teeth with sharp objects. He imitates a dentists
patient as well as the dentist himself, *imitation* and *mimicry*.
He departs from the cool and collected Cosby that we know to
become a blithering idiot unable to speak with a mouth full of
Novocain, *character contradiction*. And the entire piece is a
statement that dentists don't conduct themselves the way they
should, *satire*. The only level of comedy that Cosby refuses to
resort to is obscenity and profanity, and for this reason he has
been a splendid role model to hundreds of comedians.

Some people put down low comedy, saying that it has no real
value compared to high comedy, with its social message and
biting commentary. They say that most low comedy is just
juvenile attempts at humor using dirty jokes to get embarrassed
laughter from the audience. Well I say to them, "Thpppppbt!"
Both types of comedy can be just as satisfying. In fact, some

people seek out low forms of comedy because their daily life requires them to ponder all day about weighty issues such as politics, earning a living, and raising a family. They need a relaxing outlet that doesn't require a lot of concentrated thought. A quick look at the overwhelming success of some of the silly comedy movies made today shows that these people are not alone.

> *The more complex the mind,*
> *the greater the need for the simplicity of play.*
> A quote from some old Star Trek episode.
> (The one where they beam down to a
> planet and get whatever they want just
> by thinking about it. Cool!)

Chapter 14
"My wife never gets my jokes"
GENDER AND LAUGHTER

Women! Can't live __with__ 'em, can't live __near__ 'em.
Richard W. Rentfrow

I don't know why you're laughing. I think this show is stupid.
Every girlfriend I ever dated

No serious discourse on the nature of humor would be complete if I didn't try to break up a few good relationships by discussing the fundamental differences in humor between men and women. The age-old saying that the difference between men and women is that "Men think the Three Stooges are funny and women think they're stupid" has more truth to it than you might think. As a comedian I can attest to the difficulty in finding material that spans the gulf between the sexes. This gap is as a product of many years of social and psychological conditioning. Women and men are raised, for the most part, with different expectations and limitations. These variances in environment, along with differences in psychological make-up, create very specific conditions for the acceptance of humor.

There are many cases where differences in humor stem more from individual taste than from gender. And many times it is difficult to see any difference at all, especially if you were to watch a polished professional entertainer. Years of training and experience helps comedians develop material that appeals to both sexes. However, as we have seen by examining the Pyramid of Comedy, an entire roomful of people may be laughing, but they may be laughing for difference reasons. While some audience members enjoy the physicality of the performance, others may enjoy the recognition of themselves in the story. Others may discern a satirical stab at a social institution. In general, men and women in America experience the same lifestyle and culture, and like a tree, the further you move away from the trunk the more varied the differences. Many comedians spend much of their time dealing with the trunk of the tree so that they will appeal to everyone. As you travel out to certain branches you discover that there are some wonderful differences between men and women and their appreciation of humor.

In his book, *Men Are From Mars, Women Are From Venus,* John Gray says that men and women have difficulties in relationships because they fail to understand exactly how the other thinks.

> *We mistakenly assume that if our partners love us, they will react and behave in certain ways—the ways we react and behave when we love someone*
> John Gray, Ph.D.

We go into a relationship with the mistaken belief that the other person approaches communication, love, and commitment the same way we do. We approach issues and concerns of daily life blindly expecting the other person to yield to our way of thinking. This leads to many misunderstandings. Arguments ensue because neither side thinks they have done anything wrong—"What did I say *now*?" When we take time to learn how the other person thinks and communicates, we eliminate many of the problems of the relationship.

Most arguments are not actually about the surface issues (who forgot what at the store, who doesn't call often enough, who stuffed a sock into who's pet poodle because the little furball wouldn't stop yapping and yapping, etc.). Arguments are most often really about what we feel is important and how we communicate those feelings to each other. Women (and I speak in the general sense) feel that family and home are the highest priority. Men also value these things, but on the priority scale of life they fall just below tickets to the Super Bowl and a riding lawnmower with a 85 horsepower Tecumseh engine, a graphite tipped mulching blade, and a rear-mounted quick-release, Teflon leaf-bag attachment.

At the beginning of the book I said that laughter is the most universal expression in the world, and it is. However, as universal as laughter is, humor is the most restricted form of communication. In order for humor to work and laughter to occur, the comedian must take into account the age, education, social background, political beliefs, religion, and moral codes of his or her audience. If a performer were to step on the audience's toes in any one of these areas, the performance would be met with sullen silence. The same is true when considering gender, but that job is tougher. A comedian may be unfamiliar with the small town where the evenings show will be, but some quick inquiries and a look through the local paper can remedy the problem. Unfamiliarity with the opposite sex can never really be cured—it can only be lived with and enjoyed (hey, you either laugh or cry). When it comes to laughter, three main conditions contribute to the gender split: *psychological make-up*, *environment*, and *social status*.

Some scholarly types have formulated interesting theories about the behavioral difference between men and women. Especially intriguing is the theory that men and women approach love and sex differently because of biophysiology. The theory is that humans developed their hormonal and physical reactions to sex eons ago as a means of personal and social survival. Early in our evolution, when humans were as much the hunted as the hunter, it was important for the man to stay emotionally detached from the woman during sex so he could be aware of any danger. When animals mate they are physically vulnerable to attack, and the vulnerability is greater if the couple is mentally unaware that a predator is approaching. So the larger stronger male took the role of "keeping one eye open" for possible attack. This explains why even today a man's sex drive diminishes immediately after the act. A man's physical response to sexual stimulation can be charted on a graph. A chart of a human males physical response to sex shows an immediate "charging" of the body upon initial stimulation. This is followed by a sharp and continuous rise during sex, until orgasm. Then a complete shut-down of the sexual response occurs. When connected to the theory that our biophysiology developed as a result of the need for survival, male sexual drop-off is not due to a lack of interest, it is a function of the autonomic nervous system. It is a physical reaction to ensure that the man stays on guard against predators. This need to guard against attack is of course no longer a concern, depending on the neighborhood you live in, but given some of the organs we still have that fell out of use centuries ago you can see that evolution doesn't always keep up to date.

Women of that time needed to ensure their own survival and the security of their babies, so it was important for them to find a mate that was strong and aggressive. Men instinctively look for women with round hips and full breasts because these physical traits indicate a good child-bearing mate. Women look for men with large muscles and an aggressive character because these traits are necessary to protect and provide for home and family. Biology dictates that we act in ways that will ensure the survival of the species. For early woman that meant protection. In order to survive during the vulnerable months of pregnancy the mother would need to keep the man nearby for protection, hence the stronger bonding nature of women. Since men needed to impregnate as many women as possible to ensure the survival of his lineage, a competitive situation could develop between women of the tribe. So it was important for the woman to make sure the man was going to stick around before allowing herself to be burdened with a child. And since women were saddled with the child after the birth, they needed to make sure the man was going to be a good provider, not an easy job during a time when there was no family court.

According to this theory, many of our modern day attitudes stem from this early evolutionary trait. Most men say they don't need emotional commitment for sex; women say they need love in order for sex to be meaningful. Of course there are changes in society that cause our biophysiology to gradually change. Men no longer need to protect women from invading hordes (frat houses not withstanding), and women are self-sufficient with or without a man. Men have taken on more responsibility as parents, and women are demanding an equal part in corporate America. Women are in the military and men watch Oprah Winfrey. But even with all these sweeping changes, the core of our physiology is largely the same. It causes us to approach mating differently, communication is trickier, and we view laughter differently.

The chemical and hormonal processes in our bodies help create our moods and attitudes. Women's hormones urge them to constantly see that the family is safe, warm, and healthy. Men's hormones drive them to achieve success, to claim victory, and to build four-wheel drive monster trucks. For these reasons it is difficult for women to find humor in violence or aggression. Harsh language, humor that demeans others, violent physical humor, all are usually the playground of men. Little boys grow up on the playground pushing and shoving, having play fights and wars, and engaging in all manner of behavior that defines their pecking order. For men, hierarchy in the tribe is extremely important. Even in a room full of mature adult males, when asked most would instantly be able to tell you who they think they could "take" in a fight. Women will delight in physical humor that displays a playful attitude or special skill such as clowns at a circus or a wonderfully choreographed farce. Shtick that is violent—The Three Stooges bashing each others heads with plumbing pipes— is met with a shake of the head and a tsk tsk tsk.

A friend of mine we'll call Ellen (because that's her name) summed up most women's feelings on physical humor by saying that she preferred the Marx Brothers to the Three Stooges. At first the two styles of comedy would appear very similar. Both employ wild gestures, energetic delivery, and precise timing, but the nature of the humor differs. The Marx Brothers rarely used violence. Both groups victimized each other as well as other characters in the performance, but the Stooges were constantly hitting, slapping, and boinging each other in the head with metal objects. The violence is so realistic that audiences today still wince when they see Moe smack Curly over the head with a tire iron. The Marx Brothers however, used silly gestures and tightly choreographed movements to generate laughter. Most men I have spoken to enjoy both styles, whereas the women draw the line at the Stooges.

In general, men are a visually stimulated animal, and women are emotionally stimulated. This fact has been used for years to explain why men can be in a long-term relationship and still find other women attractive. They love their wives dearly and mean no disrespect to the marriage, but if a cutie in a short skirt saunters by in the mall, they'll gawk. Women often say that after becoming involved with one man they lose all interest in other men. Men can not understand how women can just turn off their attraction to other men, and women can not understand why men need to look at other women when they are happy in the relationship. Which goes with the old saying, *Men fall in love with women they are attracted to, and women become attracted to the men they love.* Neither situation is "right" or "wrong," they are simple facts of life.

This phenomena does explain some of the differences in gender and comedy. Men are more prone to respond to wild physical humor for its own sake. Women generally need to see more plot involved with the physicality. Women's lack of tolerance for violent humor extends past physical comedy. The late Sam Kinison, best known for his misogynist routines and screaming delivery, found his biggest following in college-age men. Their chest-thumping cheers were loudest when Kinison went on the rampage against minority groups and women. His rock-and-roll attitude was reflected in his anything-but-subtle attacks on old girlfriends, gays, and starving Ethiopians. It is said that as men grow older their aggressive tendencies subside and the feminine side of their being surfaces. This would account for a lack of older male fans for comedians like Sam Kinison and Andrew Dice Clay.

Working hand in hand with socio-biophysiology, environment and upbringing greatly influence gender differences in comedy appreciation. For the most part, little girls are taught that it is proper to sit quietly and be polite. Loud and aggressive behavior is not at all appropriate. Little boys, on the other hand, are expected to be boisterous and assertive. Even parents who try to raise both sexes with total equality can not fully counteract the effects of society. Society stills believes that boys are loud and pushy and girls are sweet and demure. Children are very adept at sensing which behaviors will net them positive reinforcement from adults, and from each other. Being very self-centered beings with fragile egos, children are in constant need of emotional attention and approval from grown-ups. Children with brothers and sisters have to compete for attention. When children grow old enough to leave home for school during the day they are suddenly thrust into an entire roomful of children just as frightened as themselves. A whole classroom filled with buckets of emotional need. Obviously one teacher can't possibly satisfy the needs of all the children. So they are left to try to get attention any way they can. Many times in the fight for attention, children will try to get any response from an adult, positive or negative.

This delicate stage of a child's life is where a good deal of his or her comedic ability, or disability, is cemented. In the late '80s the United Way developed a social program called Success by Six. It was founded on the belief that all the traits that make up an adult human being are fully in place by age six.

All of our skills, doubts, fears, confidence, our entire self-image, is instilled by the time we reach the tender age of a kindergartner. The belief also stated that our self-image remains unchanged into adulthood. If we are given a positive self-image as a child we will achieve greater success as an adult, and if we are given a poor emotional foundation it will be very difficult to change as we mature.

What this means for comedy is this. Those who discover that humor will get them attention will zero in on it as a means of recognition. If a child makes people laugh, it is a powerful combination of control, which most children crave, and positive feedback. Even a negative outcome is worth the prize of laughter. Class clowns who get sent to the principals office consider it a fair price for getting the entire class to laugh at a fake fart noise. If little girls are taught that being funny isn't ladylike, it is a sure bet that humor will not be a big part of their adult life. However, if a little girl is unable to compete with classmates who have superior smarts or looks, the girl will say, "To heck with ladylike, I'm getting some laughs."

Environmental conditioning also plays a part in women's tendency to appreciate less aggressive forms of comedy. Most men spent their childhood playing rough-and-tumble games. Their friendships were bonded with good-natured insults and punches in the arm. As little girls were telling each other that they will be best friends forever and reading each other's most secret diaries, little boys were putting bugs into each others ears and telling jokes that involved one of three main subjects: poop, poop, and poop. Growing up with such behaviors as bonds of friendship create common sources of laughter. Boys and girls are dealt an early hand of cards that guides their humor as adults.

When we laugh we respond on an almost purely instinctive level. We also respond to the expectations placed upon us. Most people agree with the notion that girls mature faster than boys. If a little girl learns of this, she will be sure to help the cliché become true, especially since it paints her in a more positive light. What child wouldn't try to make themselves appear superior to their nemesis? So the little girl will start acting more mature because it is what is expected of her. Little boys will rebel against the notion of girls being more "adult" by acting like complete idiots. Mission accomplished. Since jokes and comedy are often seen as acts of the mischievous and childish, little girls live up to the image of being more mature than boys by not engaging in such behavior. Cracking jokes and acting silly to get laughs from friends are interpreted by girls as the immature actions of some stupid little boys. The conditions of our upbringing are a constant undercurrent, affecting our comedic maturity and tastes. As long as adults hold the notion that "boys will be boys and girls will be girls," men and women will always view comedy through different eyes. As women began to gain more respect as comedians in the 90's, the notion that "little girls didn't act that way" began to change. More and more comediennes experienced the freedom to be funny and not be labeled "one of the guys," or a "ball-busting female."

Social status has a unique effect on how people approach humor. As we have seen in earlier chapters, comedy can be an influential tool for social change, but the comedian must be very careful about content and delivery lest the powers that be find offense. The third law of laughter, laughter of superiority, dictates that there always must be a target, someone or something at which the laughter is directed. Comedians who enjoy a powerful social position need not worry about who they offend. Someone who is without such power must be very careful not to step too heavily on the wrong toes. For many centuries women have endured just such a position. Men continue to earn more money than most women for the same job. In the past men controlled the flow of money or the decisions that influence its use in the household. Until recently men were allowed to control most major decisions in society. Women had to exert their influence in subtle ways, and to make their influence effective they had to develop powers of persuasion that did not rest on the luxury of having the final word. This situation put women in the position of discerning and utilizing subtle nuances in language, attitude, and nonverbal communication. If you are in a position of lower status and you need to convince your superior of something, you will take careful note of the affect of your approach. Centuries of having to pay such close attention to communication sharpened women's abilities of observation. That's why a man and a woman can walk into a bar and the woman will immediately be able to tell you who in the room is trying to "pick up" whom. The man will be able to tell you where the bar is. If you don't need to rely on subtle communication for survival you won't develop an eye for it.

Until the early '90s, women have never really found support or recognition in the area of comedy. The comedy boom of the late '80s opened the door to comedians of all types and backgrounds, including women, but before then comedy was strictly a man's game. Female comedians were the exception, not the rule. It is no secret that the prevailing opinion of the day was that men were simply better comedians; they were seen to be funnier and more polished performers. No surprise considering girls were given very little support from family and friends when they exhibited any kind of comedic behavior as children. This put women at a severe disadvantage if they decided to pursue comedy as a career. A weak social position left them unable to fully develop what might have been an important part of their personality. This is not at all meant to say that women's personalities are lacking because they weren't allowed to follow their comedy dreams. Those women who did have a desire to be funny, in life or on stage, were simply not given the same support as men.

In my comedy classes men and women from all walks of life take the first step in discovering if they have what it takes to stand on stage and make people laugh, either as a stand-up comedian, a comedy sketch actor, or an improv troupe member. The same statistic holds true year after year, there are two funny women for every ten funny men.

Many students, men and women, come to me when they realize that they just aren't as funny as the next student in class.

They feel frustrated and helpless as to how to become as funny as the performers they admire. I give them all the same advise: be patient and understand at what point you are in your development as a comedic performer. Many people have grown up knowing that comedy is their strong suit. They rely on humor as a cornerstone of their self-image. As a result, they look at everyday humor much differently than others. If mom and dad say, "Our oldest child is a great thinker, gets real good grades." That child will latch onto that as an identity, studying and getting good grades. If the parents say, "Little tommy, boy are you good with your hands." The likely result is a carpenter in the family. If mom and dad say, "Well, we have quite a little comedian in our family." Get ready for another Jerry Seinfeld. As a result if a person who is "good with his hands" or "quite the little thinker" cracks a joke at a party and no one laughs, they have little emotional loss. They know that they are a good at other things and they draw their self-image from that. "Well, I guess I just can't tell a joke. Oh well. I'm going to be a carpenter anyway." If a comedic person tells a joke at a party and it bombs, they take it much more seriously. No one likes to think that they have a special talent only to have it fail them in front of others. So people with comedic personalities start learning at a very young age how to be perfect at being funny. They take note of what makes people laugh and what doesn't, they consciously and unconsciously lock into memory every trick that gets a laugh. By the time they reach adulthood they have a storeroom full of comedy stuff: jokes, stories, noises, facial expressions, and voices. If you are fortunate enough to have a comedian as a friend, you have probably heard these stories and jokes a few hundred times, because to a comedian, each new acquaintance is a chance to get more laughs with his favorite stuff.

If these comedic people decide on comedy as a career, they are jumping into it with a lifetime of practice. Their comedic skills are honed from daily observation and exercise. Some people decide late in life that they want to try comedy. These people are starting at square one, a very frustrating place to be. They have spent their entire life becoming the best engineer, mother, computer programmer, or bartender possible, and now they are switching gears. They are in the position of having to develop the same skills other comedians have been working on their entire lives. And it's more difficult for adults to fail at comedy because they are not used to investing time and commitment in something that doesn't offer immediate payback. They are accustomed to a cause and effect relationship. If they go to a gym and exercise, they will lose weight. If they go to a skiing school, they will learn how to ski. Trying to rejuvenate comedy genes that have been laying dormant for decades is a monumental task, and one that does not produce quick results. I tell these students that they have to go through the same process that the comedic personalities did, and it might take just as long. So, if they're starting out at the tender age of 35, they have a lot of catching up to do. Add in the fact that adults learn new skills at a slower rate than children and it can be quite a wall to climb.

Women have traditionally been put on the back burner of comedy. Their social status has neither allowed them to enter the world of comedy nor given them the power to change societies views on women and comedy. They were, in a sense, told to shut up and sit down while the men talked. So they learned to appreciate humor from the outside. They could watch and enjoy, but they could be funny themselves only in the right settings (usually only with their close friends). And it wasn't just the men who kept women from displaying comedic personalities. On the contrary, women can be much harsher toward each other than the treatment they get from men. Actually, in most households it was the woman who laid the guidelines for good behavior. The man may have had final say in "big" decisions, but the woman was left the day-to-day task of raising the children. This gave them power to instill ideas of good and bad behavior. Women decided what was correct humor and what was in poor taste. They did this using their sense of moral decency and proper social etiquette. As the old saying goes, "Men make the laws, women make the morals." With mothers telling their daughters that loud and brash behavior wasn't acceptable, it is no wonder women have such a hurdle to jump when they decide to be funny. Thank God such ideas are becoming a thing of the past, or we would not be blessed with the talents of Lilly Tomlin, Ellen DeGeneres, Tracey Ullman, Gilda Radner, and Roseanne Barr.

Social status not only affects a persons ability to be funny, it can also affect what a person appreciates as being humorous. Women have had to spend so many years not biting the hand that fed them they developed attitudes that reflecting an underdog status. The result was a confirmation of the conditions set in motion by biophysiology and upbringing—a disdain for humor that attacked defenseless targets. Harsh comedians like Andrew Dice Clay and Sam Kinison were the favorite of college-aged men, but were hated by women. Years of enduring a lower social status made women especially sensitive to attacks on gays, women, minorities, in general the underdog. Young men loved Clay and Kinison because they put forth the type of comedy that called for men to be men and women to stay out of the way. Such performances more closely resembled a white men's rally than a comedy show.

Years of being in power has given men an appreciation for humor free from worry. Men are more often apt to laugh openly in public. They are the first to bellylaugh in a comedy club or theatre, a sign of social power. A group in a society that enjoys power takes opportunities to display that power. Loud vocalizations are common, whether it be boisterous debates over favorite sports teams at a bar, or guffaws of laughter at a funny story. Social power also carries with it the lack of worry about offending others. Whereas women had to protect their ladylike image by displaying a quiet demeanor, men could engage in raucous behavior and be challenged by no one. To this day there are couples of men and women in comedy clubs where the women unconsciously check to see if the man is laughing before they will allow themselves to giggle quietly.

The conditions that affect men and women as they laugh are, fortunately, subject to change. For the most part we are all human and we find laughter in common sources. Certain conditions can be overridden or rechannelled; little boys who are raised in a quiet household and taught to be courteous and polite may override the biophysiological urge to laugh at aggressive comedy. There are scores of women who, regardless of their gender, love a good raunchy joke. As the "politically correct" movement took hold in the early '90s, the lines of good taste and appropriate humor became more clearly defined. What was once pooh-poohed as mildly offensive was instead attacked as subversive, violent, and counterproductive to positive social change.

As women gain more power in society their appreciation of comedy changes as well as their participation in it. Women in the '90s are rethinking what is "ladylike behavior." they are taking jobs and hobbies heretofore reserved for the male of the species. Politics, heavy construction, bodybuilding, karate, boxing, football, and hockey are making way for what used to be called the weaker sex. Personally, I've trained as a martial artist for over twenty years, and the bruises to both my body and ego from the women have never led me to believe they were the weaker sex.

The artist formerly known as Prince (or is it the artist formerly known as the artist formerly known as Prince?) has ushered in what he calls "The New Power Generation." And women have begun to reflect that power in their comedy. A mere few years can see drastic changes in humor. Not long ago, comediennes like Roseanne Barr Arnold, Janeane Garofalo, Margaret Smith, Judy Tenuta, and Sandra Bernhard would have been dismissed as "too harsh." Now they are embraced as they expose the hypocrisy and inequity of a male dominated world.

Before, women had to sit quietly as male comedians took pot shots at their entire gender with jokes about mothers-in-law, women drivers, stupid wives, and the mechanically inept girl. Women are still quick to laugh generously at their own expense, as are men, but will not stand for broad dismissals of their sex as a whole. If a joke reflects an honest, yet good-natured observation about female behavior, both men and women enjoy the humor. If the joke takes the antiquated route of "Hey, aren't women stupid?" women would just as soon not hear it. Given the publics need for ever-new approaches to comedy, the intolerance for wide-sweeping generalities about women may also be a reflection of our need to hear something new and different.

The interesting thing about men and women and their changing social status is its inconsistency. When groups within a culture experience change, as men and women have in America, there are just as many hold outs for the old ways as there are proponents for the new. As much as women have banded together to wrestle power from the men, they still attack each other will equal voracity. Just as many women as men still tell "dumb blonde" jokes. Centuries of psychological and physiological conditioning don't die easily. As I talk to men and women about their comedic tastes and observe the reactions of audiences, I find that thoughtful subtle humor is still a favorite of women, and men still laugh louder.

I should clarify that just because men laugh louder and more boldly, this doesn't mean that they laugh more often. They laugh differently and sometimes for different reasons. In most everyday life situations, women laugh more than men. Robert Provine, the professor who studied ape laughter and contagious laughter, noted a marked difference in male and female responses to everyday humor. We often laugh when we are telling friends a funny story. How much we laugh in comparison to our audience depends on our gender. Our gender also affects what kind of response we can expect from our listeners. In turn, gender will affect our response if we are the audience. Provine discovered that in ordinary conversation the speaker, whether male or female, laughed 46 percent more often than the listener while telling a funny story. If a male is speaking, male and female audience members laugh more frequently than for female speakers. Female speakers are less likely to get laughter from males than from females. Basically, a male speaker will laugh slightly more than his male audience, a female speaker will laugh slightly more than her female audience. A male speaker will laugh slightly *less* than his female audience (about seven percent), and a male audience member will laugh *significantly* less than his female speaker. In fact, female speakers laugh 127 percent more often than their male audience.

Studies show that the trend of males being the chief laugh producers and women being the leading laughers extends to most cultures. This is due to the fact that women are raised to fill a supportive role in society. Women are generally taught to be more polite and nurturing than men. If a speaker is telling a humorous story it is only polite to laugh. If the speaker is laughing while speaking, women sense the need to support the atmosphere being established and will support it by laughing themselves. Laughter can also be seen as a form of submission if it is done to support another and not to establish power. If a man were to laugh with someone in a social setting it would be an act of transferring power to the other person. Many men unconsciously guard their power and are reluctant to release it, especially to women, which would explain the discrepancy in male and female audiences laughter.

There are many factors at work in the creation of a laughing human of either gender. To understand the origin of each other's laughter can certainly go a long way in helping to bridge the gap of the sexes. Just don't expect women to ever make fart noises with their armpits.

Part III
MODERN COMEDY

Chapter 15
ANATOMY OF A JOKE

All truly wise thoughts have been thought already thousands of times; but to make them truly ours, we must think them over again honestly, until they take root in our personal experience.
Goethe

I can't think of any new ideas!
Almost every comedian alive today

A college sociology professor of mine once claimed that parenthood was the one job in the world for which people received the least amount of training. He is right that anyone can become a parent with no previous experience, no interview, no test to pass, but he is wrong about parenthood being the least prepared vocation. Parents-to-be read volumes of books and get advice from doctors, parents, siblings, and friends with babies of their own. They'll prepare for months for the new arrival, and by the time the baby is brought home from the hospital the parent's heads are crammed with the words of Dr.

Spock, advice from talk shows, and great-aunt Edna's phone number just in case.

Comedians, on the other hand, jump on to the stage with nothing more that the hopes of making people laugh. Ask anyone of them what it is that actually makes a person laugh and you'll get a blank stare. In a television interview, Jerry Seinfeld was asked, "What makes something funny?" His reply was, "I don't know. I can tell when something's funny, but not why." Even though Mr. Seinfeld claims not to know what actually makes people laugh, he and thousands of other stand-up comedians and comedic actors use specific techniques of comedy to make their writing and performance more effective. A good many techniques are known to comedians and writers, and are passed down through the generations like favorite recipes. These techniques make use of the very laws of comedy that I have laid out in this book, often without the writer even being aware that the law exists.

If you watch a stand-up comedian performing an act, you begin to sense a rhythm to the delivery of the material. The audience picks up this rhythm unconsciously and begins to respond to it, sometimes laughing before the joke is finished. Even though every comedian's timing and delivery is unique, they all possess a rhythm that sustains the pace of their act. This delivery relies on the circumstances discussed earlier in this book. This set of circumstances guides the audience to the source of humor - surprise, recognition, and superiority. All comedy material follows a formula that takes advantage of these conditions, whether the comedy is on the stage or on the street. The formula is simple to understand, but difficult to execute. In order for comedy material to generate a laugh it must have a *premise*, a *set up*, and a *punchline.*

The *premise* is the topic of conversation, the theme of the material. It lets the audience know the focus of the story or joke. The *set up* is all the information the audience needs to know to follow the story and understand the plot. The *punchline* is the funny line or unexpected conclusion. In comedy presentations a story or routine may have one punchline at the end, or have small punchlines scattered throughout which lead to a big conclusion. Let's look at the elements of premise, set up, and punchline more closely.

The Premise

The premise seems to be the simplest element, but is often overlooked when analyzing why an event or story is or is not funny. The premise, or theme, is only funny when it has some amount of importance or recognition to the listener. For the same reason New Yorkers don't make jokes about Utah, comedians can't rely on topics that are of no interest to the audience.

If you watch a bad performer, you can sense when he or she is stretching a premise to force a comedic idea. I saw a young comedian spend a good deal of time talking about how stupid the song "White Wing Dove" was and why it shouldn't be on the radio. His premise was based entirely on the song, but he failed to take into account that the song was long past being popular and was no longer played on the radio. He had probably thought of the joke long ago, waited for the courage to try comedy, and pulled out all his old ideas including the "White Wing Dove" joke. The joke never got a laugh and he couldn't understand why. He tried reworking the joke for many months, but never got a laugh with it. He failed to realize that his premise was outdated and of no interest to the audience, and no amount of rewriting would make them care about the song again.

You can also see when a comedian has thought of a "funny idea" and has built a joke around it because the premise is not a common experience of the audience. Instead of talking about experiences we can relate to, these comedians look at everyday things and try to *make them funny*. "Hey, what about those parking meters? Aren't they stupid? What's up with that?" They have missed the importance of selecting themes and ideas that actually affect the audience.

The importance of the premise dictates why comedians on TV must use very general themes. There are only so many themes that are common enough to everyone that they will generate laughter. This is especially true for a performer entertaining millions of people through television. If you visit a local club you can see how comedians use the power of selective premise to their advantage. Local issues are good fodder for an astute comedian. In fact, it is common for traveling comedians to ask the hotel clerk or waitress in the town they are performing to let them in on the local gossip.

Knowing what's on everyone's mind gives them ammunition for that night's show. Most towns have similar enough issues that comedians need only change the names in routines they already have and they're up to date for the new city. It's no different than a rock star saying, "Are you ready to rock Tulsa?" to get applause. Television comedians can't look into the camera and say, "Let's laugh America!" They must rely on the common experiences we all share–driving, working, paying taxes, and dealing with family. If a comedian selects a premise that is a common experience of the audience, the foundation of a good joke has been laid.

The Set Up

The set up provides a very important function. Without a good set up, the story will not flow or make sense, and it will not provide a good basis for the punchline. We have all heard a friend tell a joke, and he was so eager to get to the punchline that he either rushed through the story or left out important information, only to have to go back and fill it in later, long after we stopped caring about the joke and just wanted to get back to dinner. We have also heard a friend tell a joke, but was so meandering in the story that we couldn't follow along.

True to its name, the set up is the part of the story that *sets* the audience *up*, and guides their line of thought. Laughter can not occur unless the audience is surprised. In order to be surprised the audience must be thinking in a clear direction. They must build a set of expectations about the story, and it is

191

the comedian's job to make sure those expectations lead away from the punchline, so that when it is delivered the surprise will cause laughter.

Sometimes it is easy to guide the audiences line of thought. Since most of us experience life in the same way, we tend to look at the world the same. If a comedian began describing a trip to the grocery store, we unconsciously think ahead and finish the scenario. If the comedian said, "I went to the grocery store the other day...." we would think, "...*bought eggs, went through checkout, bagged groceries, heavy bag, walked to car....*" We are actually helping the comedian's set up by thinking along the lines of a typical grocery store trip, so when the comedian gets to the line about tripping and falling into the produce sprayer and getting a free shower, we are surprised and laugh. Comedians count on all of us to think in terms of the norm, only then are we easily surprised.

There are times when the comedian has a difficult time guiding our thoughts in a typical direction. People who are fans of comedy and visit clubs often are accustomed to having stories and jokes delivered with a surprise ending, so they begin to think in non-linear directions. It is almost as if they are unconsciously trying to get to the end of the joke before the comedian. It is at these times when a comedian has the most difficulty getting laughs. Veteran comedians say that the most important goal for any performer is to *control the audience.*

There is another strict requirement for a good set up: **keep it short.** As the character Polonius says in Shakespeare's *Hamlet*, "...brevity is the soul of wit...." Shakespeare knew that if you draw out the set up too long the audience will either guess the punchline before you deliver it, or worse yet, they'll become so bored they won't care about the joke anymore. It is because the audience unconsciously thinks ahead that the need to be concise is so strong. *The listener always thinks faster that you can speak.* There is no way anyone can speak faster than the human mind can process the information, and the brain needs something to do to occupy the spare time. So it wanders around, making shopping lists, arranging tomorrow's work schedule, speeding up the breathing and heartbeat to accommodate for the cute waitress that just walked by, and jumping ahead of the comedian and guessing at a few punchlines.

The fact that the brain skips ahead and fills in the blanks is why amateur comedians talk so fast: it is the only technique they have to stay ahead of the audience. Performers with years of experience have the luxury of slowing down their delivery because they have mastered writing and delivering material so that the audience can never guess the ending.

Absolutely no more information can be included in the set up than is absolutely necessary. The audience is so fickle with its attention, and so quick to jump ahead of the performer that extra information jeopardizes the speed of delivery. Extraneous facts can also make the audience think the joke is about the wrong part of the story. Extra information either leads the audience down the wrong thought path or gives away the ending. Good comedians look over their material after the first few trials and look for any single word that can be removed without ruining the joke. This is called *tightening up the act* and sharpens the material immeasurably. A comedian with a concise clear set-up that gets to the point quickly has created a solid ramp for the audience to get to the punchline.

The Punchline

The punchline is very tricky to write and to deliver. It must work in perfect harmony with the set up. It must take the expectations developed by the set up and surprise the audience with a twist, thus creating a joke. Usually the punchline achieves its goal by creating two things: *contrast* and *exaggeration*. Contrast is a basic element of all comedy. The pairing of two unconnected ideas has long been recognized by scholars of comedy as a necessary component of humor. The contrast in a joke is usually between the set up and the punchline. If the set up is vague, the punchline should be specific; if the set up is factual, the punchline should be fictional. The contrast can also be contained within the delivery of the punchline, such as a very spiteful comment being made with a smiling face, or a performer with a seemingly goofy character may deliver a line that actually has intelligent satire buried within. If the set up is delivered with a happy, cheerful attitude, then the punchline is delivered with a surprising anger.

Contrast is important for a good punchline because it is the quickest way to surprise the audience. Since most people have experienced a variety of situations in life, it is difficult to create a story that will take them completely by surprise. Creating a contrast of two unconnected ideas surprises the audience because there are two many variations to be able to have thought of them all before the delivery of the punchline.

Exaggeration, the other element of a good punchline, is also important for comedy. It is what provides the sense of fun and light-heartedness needed for laughter to occur. If a friend told us that it took 20 minutes to get served at a restaurant, we would not see much humor in the situation because it is not an unusual wait. If the friend said that he waited so long for the waiter he needed a walker to get to the buffet, we would laugh at the exaggeration of his predicament.

If used carefully, exaggeration provides the spice that distinguishes humor from simply reporting the news of the day. If used to excess, exaggeration can expose someone who is too eager to get a laugh. Exaggeration must be doled out with care. A comedian is never quite sure how far to take embellishment in a story. If she starts out saying it took two hours to get her foot unstuck from a bathtub drain, the audience will laugh. If she says it took two days, they may laugh harder. If she says it took two months, they may not laugh at all. Many times comedians are left to simple trial and error to determine how far an exaggeration can go before it enters the not-funny zone. They will start out with a small exaggeration for a joke and increase the exaggeration each time they tell it, monitoring carefully the exact amount that gets the most laughs. Two hours stuck in a bathtub is plausible, two days is ridiculous, two months is so impossible we can't do what is necessary for laughter, *imagine in our minds the comedian actually caught in the predicament.*

It is important to remember that the audience is relying heavily on the laughter of recognition to find humor in a story. This is where the concept of *suspension of disbelief* is important. When we listen to story told by a friend in a non-comedic setting we employ built-in reality checks. We believe what we think is real and know to disbelieve what is false. Our ever-present analyzers process everything we hear and warn us of the fake stuff. This is a good protective measure. It keeps us from buying too many worthless gadgets from traveling salesmen. The trouble is that it is not very fun. *Suspension of disbelief* means the audience will believe situations of a more fantastic nature for the time they are watching a performance because they know it is for the sake of entertainment. This happens in comedy as well as drama, romance, science fiction, etc.

A comedian must be careful not to stretch suspension of disbelief too far. If you say it took two days to get unstuck from the drain, they can <u>envision</u> you sitting in the bathtub for two days, stupidly waiting for help. When you cross into two years it becomes less plausible and harder to envision, and the laughter of recognition is lost. So, even though a situation is grossly exaggerated, it must still seem somewhat realistic to the audience. It is as if the audience is saying, "We are willing to suspend disbelief to help you out with your story, but don't take advantage of us." In this way, the audience gives up just enough control to have fun and laugh, but not enough that the comedian can appear to be *trying* for a laugh. In order for the audience to laugh at the bathtub incident, they must believe that the comedian actually lived it, therefore they must believe that the comedian believes it. When the comedian over-exaggerates the story the audience immediately senses that he isn't *living* the story and they refuse to laugh. This is why comedians are always told, "Never laugh at your own jokes." If a performer laughs at his own material, it no longer appears to the audience that the comedian has honestly lived what he is saying, and the humor is lost. In this way, the audience is actually demonstrating that they *want* to suspend disbelief, because they want to believe the fantastic things the comedian is saying. The comedian knows that the audience is on his side, but doesn't know just how far. No wonder comedy is hard.

Techniques of Writing Comedy

"Stick with me kid. I'll show ya da ropes."

Over the years, comedy writers have developed techniques for getting laughs on a consistent basis. These techniques work because they adhere to the principles of laughter. Some techniques are so common that they are over-used, which is why some forms of comedy, such as bad sit-coms, are so predictable. We recognize the techniques and see that the obvious attempt is for a laugh, so we resist. If used effectively, however, the techniques are sound methods for guiding the audiences line of thought and ensuring a laugh at just the right place. Although more commonly discussed today in terms of stand-up comedy—the *style de jour*—these writing techniques are used in all forms of comedic performance because they employ the basic laws inherent to all humor.

The Rule of Three

The Rule of Three has been a standard in comedy for decades. The rule dictates that if the first two items in a list are normal, the third should be unusual. *"I took along the normal things for my honeymoon: a nice suit, a bottle of wine, a gun."* The Rule of Three takes full advantage of two principles we have discussed about humor: *the audience thinks fast*, and *humor thrives on the unexpected.*

Tim Allen: (to a woman who just complimented him at a baby shower)
"Say, can I get you anything? A cold drink? Some dip? A condominium?"

> "Home Improvement"
> United Paramount Network

Since the audience is always thinking fast, the Rule of Three is effective because of its brevity. By the time the performer mentions the second normal item in the list, the audience already senses a pattern, and has thought of a number of alternatives for the next item. An unusual third item creates surprise since the audience is expecting a normal third item.

For the Rule of Three to work it is very important that there be no more than three items (save for the exceptions noted in the next section). If the list included four items, with the first three being normal, the audience would not only have discerned the pattern, they would have enough time to sense that the comedian is leading them to a joke. They would be ahead of the comic waiting for her to get to the punchline. The worst place for a comedian to be is *behind* the audience. *"I took along the normal things on my honeymoon, a nice suit, a bottle of wine, some flowers..."* By the time the joke gets to "some flowers" the audience is already thinking, "we get it, get to the joke!"

The Rule of Three is also a feeling. It applies to the build up to a punchline. It can be a quick list or an entire conversation. See how Jack Benny uses the Rule of Three in an argument with Phil, a character on his radio show.

Jack: Oh, hello Phil.

Phil: Hiya Jackson. How's the boy?

Jackson? Ha, ha, you know Phil it's cute the way you call me that every week. Say, what's this gag I hear about you getting your own program?

It's not a gag. You and I have been fighting so much lately that I thought it'd be better to call it quits.

Oh, that's silly.

Silly nothing. You're just tough to get along with and that's all.

Who me?

Yes you. You're always flying off the handle.
I am not, I'm sweet and lovable.   (Level 1)
And you're always yelling and shouting at me.
Shouting at you!   (Level 2)
And you're always losing your temper.
WHY YOU BAGGY-EYED INGRATE, I NEVER LOSE MY
TEMPER AND YOU KNOW IT! I LOVE YOU, YOU RAT!
          (Level 3)

The Rule of Three also incorporates another comedy technique, lists.

Lists

Lists are effective in providing the most important element of the set up to a joke, *guiding the audience's thinking.* If the comedian begins listing off items of any kind, a grocery list, holidays, things to hate about winter, we are invariably drawn to follow the line of thinking. Very few people will deviate from the list while listening to the comedian because they are afraid they would lose the line of thought and miss the joke. This phenomenon of human thought is used to a comedian's advantage. It helps provide a smooth flow to the act. The audience's tendency to follow the comedians line of thought makes the transition from one subject to another much easier. By following the comedian, the audience decreases the mental effort needed to enjoy the performance, thus giving the comedian greater control over the direction the audience is thinking.

The Rule of Three is a manifestation of the list phenomenon in that it is a quick means of guiding the audiences thought pattern. The two techniques differ however, in that not all lists need to be confined to three items to be funny. Sometimes it is the nature of the list itself that causes laughter. In the movie, *LA Story* by Steve Martin, a group of friends ordering coffee at a restaurant incorporates list humor:

#1: I'll have a decaf coffee.

#2: I'll have a Decaf espresso.

#3: I'll have a double-decaf cappuccino.

#4: Do you have any decaffeinated coffee ice cream?

#5: I'll have a double-decaffeinated half-caff, with a twist of lemon.

#2: I'll have a twist of lemon.

#1: I'll have a twist of lemon.

#3: I'll have a twist of lemon.

#4: I'll have a twist of lemon.

LA Story

The humor from this list comes from a number of different sources. The sheer number and variety of coffees available in restaurants and coffeehouses borders on the absurd. The fact that each guest was so particular about their own coffee is funny in the light that each order is not that different from the other. If you were to watch the scene instead of reading it, the speed of the ordering is so fast that it almost sounds mechanical. The characters seem not to control their own behavior. If you to watch the scene in the context of the movie you would see the satirical statement about the power of trends in Los Angeles. The list also grows in absurdity as the ordering continues. And finally, it is humorous to see everyone jump on the "lemon twist bandwagon" after customer number five places his order. Watchful viewers would also see that number five ordered a twist of lemon, but didn't order any coffee.

On a side note, the movie also contains some examples of other comedy techniques discussed earlier. In the chapters on physical comedy and obscenity we saw how a conversation that is high-minded and ethereal could be made humorous if a sudden reference were made to something base, common, or physical. In *LA Story*, Martin's character is guided by an omnipotent highway sign. It is the kind of sign that spells out words by lighting a field of small light bulbs. The sign seems to be all-knowing, silently giving Martin sage advise about his career and relationships. At the end of the movie when Martin has all he wants—a good job and the woman of his dreams—he asks if there's any gift he could give the sign by way of thanks. After a short pause the omniscient, all-powerful sign flashes back, "I want to get cable TV." During the closing scene of the movie the sign makes a final stab at the movie mentality of Los Angeles by flashing, "What I really want is to **direct**."

Back to lists. In my own stand-up comedy act I tell the audience how I grew up as a very wimpy young boy. My classmates called me all the nasty names you could imagine. In my act I start listing off the typical names we all used on the playground: nerd, wuss, geek, dork, pinhead, etc. The laughter at the beginning of the list is the laughter of recognition. Since we don't use these names on a daily basis anymore it is fun to hear them again, bringing us back to our own days on the playground. There is also the humor of contrast, since these are childish names being said by an adult in an adult setting. Then the audience gets a surprise. Instead of recalling a few names and leaving it at that, I go on and on, building the list longer and longer and increasing the intensity of the delivery until the last name is shouted at the top of my lungs. The list includes at least thirty names. The sheer number of names surprises the audience into laughter. The idea of me placing enough importance on childhood insults to create a list is also funny in and of itself, which brings us to the next comedy technique.

Attaching Importance to Trivia

If you were to examine most comedians, their acts largely consist of material that is considered trivial compared ·to the problems most of us face every day. Yet these comedians place great importance on these matters. They are so worked up over the stupidest things, we laugh. By doing this, the comedian allows us to access our feelings of superiority in a very direct way.

Satirical comedians use current events and political figures as fodder for social commentary. Some social issues have such importance that the comedian takes a risk that the issues are too heavy for us to find humor in them. The comedian must work extra hard to create an atmosphere of joviality to counteract the effect of what is normally a tense subject. Many times we hold back laughter just as much to avoid offending others as we do from our own indignation. If a comedian places a great deal of importance on a trivial matter however, we get the opportunity to laugh at his stupidity with no risk of offending anyone. A wonderful example of trivial humor comes from the comedian Sinbad and his piece about going to a McDonald's restaurant.

You've all been to McDonald's, right? Tell me this, they have not changed the menu at McDonald's in 55 years. Not one change in 55 years, but every time we go there they say "Can I help you?" and we say "Aaaaah, just a minute. I waaaaant...let me see...aaaah" What the hell we starin' at the menu for?...And I hate it when they forget to put your fries in the bag. You be drivin' home just waiting to get at them fries. You got that little french fry drool dribblin down your neck, and you reach in the bag next to you AND THEY FORGOT TO PUT THE FRIES IN!

To watch Sinbad you would think that getting french fries was the most important thing in the world. His rage over the loss of the fries is so ridiculous we can't help but laugh. Laughter is our way of saying, "Get a life!"

Jerry Seinfeld is also famous for being able to make a routine about any subject. He continually surprises the audience by spending large amounts of time talking about things that are of absolutely no importance. In fact, his sit-com, *Seinfeld,* was known for being the first television show to be about…nothing. In one routine he spends a solid five minutes talking about what happens to the one sock that is always missing after you do your laundry.

George Carlin explained the role of comedians to his audience one night by saying, "We all have a job to do. You have your job, and I have mine. My job is to think up goofy shit. That's my job. Thinking up goofy shit, and reminding you about it. 'Cause you knew it was there, you just forgot about it."

If comedians spent their time talking about heavy issues, their art would be lost to most of us. One of the reasons we go to see comedy in first place is to escape from the depressing events of the real world. A comedian who places importance on trivia not only puts our lives in perspective, but helps us forget about real issues for a little while.

<u>Contrast and Comparison</u>

A significant amount of comedy involves comparing dissimilar ideas or events. Aristotle once wrote that humor is *"the incongruous situation that does not actually represent danger or pain."* He recognized that creating a ridiculous atmosphere and causing laughter could be accomplished by putting two unrelated ideas together. Comparing two dissimilar subjects is an efficient way to create an incongruous situation. It is common to hear comedians use a basic form of comparison, the *simile*. *"Kissing my girlfriend is like kissing a fish.*" The use of "is like" in the sentence characterizes it as a simile. Another form of comparison is the *metaphor.* A metaphor compares a literal subject to an implied one, or uses an actual person or thing to represent an idea. A comedian I know tells a story of a little boy who was very spoiled and became angry every time his parents wouldn't let him pick a fight with the neighborhood children. This little boy figured out that he could rub another little boy's face in the dirt as long as he told his parents that the boy was picking on a much smaller friend. As the story continues the audience begins to see that the little boy is a metaphor for the President and the parents are a metaphor for Congress. It wasn't a funny bit—that's why I didn't mention the comedians name—but it does illustrate the technique. (Lay off. They can't all be hilarious.)

The technique of contrast and comparison is so deeply embedded in humor that theorists from every generation make mention of it in one form or another. In 1963 the writer David H. Monro formed his "10 Classes of Humor." One class was *Importing into one situation what belongs to another.* Maurice Charney in his book, Comedy High and Low created 6 areas of comedy, one being *The Ironic*, or the humor of opposites and reversals. Remember Henri Bergson and his *mechanical encrusted upon the living* theory? All of these theories involve a contrast between two dissimilar ideas or events.

Comparisons in comedy are effective in creating laughter because they always catch the audience off guard. When the comedian begins speaking about a particular subject it is almost impossible for the audience to think ahead and consider every possible funny comparison. Therefore if the comedian can make a surprise connection between two unrelated topics the audience will more easily laugh. The danger in the use of comparisons lies in the timing of the "discovery" for the audience, and the relevance of the issue at hand. Many times the comparisons comedians make are of such dissimilar topics that the audience must stretch its imagination to the limit to see the connection. If it takes too long for the connection to be made the audience has had to think too hard and the spirit of spontaneity is gone, and so is the laughter. This illustrates an important rule of comedy: *the longer the Set-Up, the bigger the Punchline.* If a comedian must take a long time to set up his joke, the audience is being asked to stretch it's attention and imagination. The pay-off must be large in order to justify the extra brain work. The moment of discovery in comparisons must be immediate as well. If a comedian makes a very clever comparison about a subject that the audience doesn't care about there will be no laughter. This need for relevance is directly related to the premise and the importance of recognition.

Coincidentally, the story of the little boy was not very successful in creating laughter for those very two reasons. One problem was that the audience had to think too long to make the connection between the little boy and the president. Another problem was that audiences had heard almost every satirical stab at presidents—the little boy story was weak by comparison. To create a good punchline more exaggeration was needed to really surprise the audience.

Comparisons are a favorite of comedians because they can take so many different forms. This makes the technique easy to include in different types of acts, no matter what the comedian's attitude, style, or delivery. Take, for instance, the different types of comparison below:

People are always asking me why I harp on the JFK assassination so much. "Let it go" they say, "It's been decades. Let it drop already." Yeah it was a long time ago. So what? Okay, I'll stop talking about JFK if you stop talking about Jesus. Talk about a subject with a long shelf life.

> Bill Hicks
> Los Angeles Comedian

*My dad is not known for his...let's say, racial tolerance. He went to see a play in Wisconsin where he lives. It was a multicultural adaptation of A Christmas Carol. He came home and said, "It was a great play. And you know what? Bob Cratchett was played by a white guy, and Tiny Tim was played by a black guy, **and you hardly even noticed!**" Mighty white of him to say so, isn't it? I could see having a hard time if the characters were played by...different species. Like Scrooge being played by a duck, Tiny Tim by a sheep. **That** would be hard. It would be tough to get past the accents. "God bless us everyone, baaaa."*

> Jackie Kashian, LA Comedian

David Monro's *Importing into one situation what belongs in another* theory is an interesting use of comparison although he was not the first to develop this theory. Many scholars of comedy use it in one form or another. For some philosophers comparison is the essence of comedy, for others it is merely one category of many—a comedy *e pluribus unum*. Without a doubt it is a major ingredient in creating laughter.

Cartoonists will often use the technique of importing one situation into another. Animals will be given human characteristics, cavemen will discuss mathematical theories about the wheel, dogs will play poker (god I wish I had that poster). We also laugh when animals are given human characteristics, in this way we assign to animals the same frailties we find amusing in ourselves. By doing so we create a paradox, whereas we laugh when humans seem not in control (Henri Bergson's *mechanical encrusted upon the living* theory), the animals appear comical in a human situation where they are given the appearance of having more control than they normally do. Even if they do not have physical control over their situation, they have the mental control to possess attitudes and opinions concerning their situation. And the more "uncool" the animal, the funnier it is for them to have any power. Gary Larson, creator of "The Far Side" cartoons was very fond of putting cows and chickens into human situations. It is not only funny to see animals in human circumstances, but we see how foolish our own actions are by having them performed by stupid animals.

209

Call Back

A call back is a reference to something said or done previously in the performance. It usually happens after a punchline is delivered and the performance has progressed in an entirely different direction. Suddenly, in the middle of a totally unrelated topic, the comedian makes a connection to the earlier punchline. The audience sees the connection to the previous joke and the contrast causes laughter.

Incorporating call backs into a stand-up act, play, or comedy performance is challenging because it requires more thought and planning than most other comedy techniques. It is not easy to find the common thread between two unrelated topics and weave them together without seeming obvious. I use a form of call back in my act while doing what comedians call "crowd rap" (when the comedian breaks from their normal act to talk to the audience). I often talk to people about their lives; what they do for a living, whether they are married, if they have children, and so on. As comedians often do, I find humor in peoples occupations. There is usually one person in the audience with a very peculiar job, a tooth molder for example. Quite some time after I've finished with crowd rap and have continued my act I perform a favorite routine of mine, a scene depicting a man trying to start his car on a freezing Minnesota winter morning. The car won't start no matter what I do. After several minutes of fighting I scream that I have to get to work at the *tooth mold* factory.

The sudden connection to a previous joke always brings laughter—for a number of reasons. One reason of course, is surprise. The audience is following the line of thought being presented—starting a car in winter—so when I slip in a previous reference the audience is caught off guard. Another is that the call back creates a connection between two entirely different themes, comparison. No audience member would watch the car-starting bit and think, "I'll bet he's going to connect this car routine with the tooth-molding guy." The routine has the certainty of surprise built in. Another reason the call back is funny is sarcasm. My repeating the occupation brings attention to its oddity. It is a good-natured stab taken at the audience member who molds teeth for a living, superiority. The audience is laughing as much *at* him as they are *with* me.

Tag

A tag is a funny line said after the punchline which is as funny or funnier than the punchline itself. Many performers deliver their material so well that it seems like one punchline follows another, each one funnier than the first. The laughter builds and builds until a climax is reached and the audience is in laughter-pain. What the comedian is doing is adding tag lines to jokes—making two or more punchlines for one set up. Tags are a very effective use of a joke, since it is easier to build a laugh on top of another than it is to generate the initial laugh.

Man talking on a phone *"Mrs. Johnson, just how fast was the car going when your driving instructor fell out?* (audience laughs) *He...he didn't fall, he jumped.* (audience laughs harder)
Bob Newhart
The Button-Down World of Bob Newhart

It is interesting to note that the comedian who uses a tag line is really playing a game of one-up with him or herself. We've all been out with the gang for a night of fun when the conversation turned to sarcastic jabs at each other. It seems there is always one person in the group who has to have the last word. He tries to top the last zinger thrown and come out as king of the hill. This person usually loses a lot of friends and has no place to go for Thanksgiving dinner. A comedian who uses tag lines is keeping one step ahead of the audience by providing a one-up to her own punchline.

Tags may be accomplished nonverbally as well. In chapter 2 on Physical Comedy I described a scene from the TV show "Cheers" where Cliff Clavin and his blind date stand motionless, transfixed with fear upon first meeting each other. The bar owner Sam sees that they are in need of help, so he intervenes. The first laugh comes when Sam starts the music. He thinks that he has done his job and he can now leave them alone, but he notices that they haven't taken the hint, or are too afraid to move. He walks over and whispers in Cliff's ear. We assume he's telling Cliff to wise up and dance with the woman (Tag #1). He sees that neither Cliff nor his date are moving and—as if he is moving two mannequins—he positions them in a dancing pose and pushes them together (Tag #2). Again he thinks his job is done and starts to walk away when he sees that they still aren't moving (Tag #3). He finally reaches over and nudges them so they start rocking and begin to dance (Tag #4). As with all well constructed tags, each laugh is larger than the one before.

See how Burns and Allen use the convention of storyline to set up a punchline, and how George sets Gracie up for the tag.

Gracie: During intermission there was some very exciting gossip in the powder room. Mrs. Harris said, "I wonder why Sara Treadwell didn't come to the ballet?" So I said, "Maybe she had a fight with her husband." And she said, "Oh not Sara." And I said, "I don't blame her, if he's running around with another woman." And so she said, "Poor Sara. Who'll take care of their five children?" And I said, "Well not that no- good husband of hers."

George: Oh, that sounds real exciting.

Gracie: Yes. It would be even more exciting if I knew who Sara Treadwell was. (Punchline)

George: You don't know Sara Treadwell?

Gracie: I don't even know Mrs. Harris. (Tag)

The success of Gracie's humor relied on the split second timing of both she and George. Even the slowest of deliveries, as Burns' was, needs attention to detail. Burns is known as the greatest straight man ever. His use of expressions, pauses, and reactions were the foundation upon which Gracie could build laughter. And perfectly timed set-ups provided for wonderfully effective punchlines and tags.

Attitude

An odd situation in comedy is that even though comedians strive to get a laugh every minute they're on stage, they often don't know how to react when they finally get one. This is more often true of the very inexperienced performer. He is standing on stage and the audience is laughing at a joke he just told. It is taking a while for the laughter to die down, so he can't start the next joke. He doesn't have a clue what to do in the meantime. He hasn't mastered the stage enough to be comfortable just standing there watching the audience laugh, so he makes one of two mistakes. One is to forget the audience, ignore the laughter, and launch right into the next joke. This mistake is often made by amateur comedians who have enough trouble just remembering each joke, let alone dealing with the audience. This comedian is usually completely unaware that the audience is even laughing. His heart is pounding so heavily it is drowning out everything in the room.

The other mistake is directly related to the tag, and is an absolute sin for a comedian to commit, **saying anything after the punchline that isn't funny.** Amateur comedians are often so thrown off balance by the audience's laughter that they continue to talk, but instead of going into the next routine they mumble meaningless addendums to the previous joke.

...so then I told him, "You can't do that, that's my mother." (Laughter begins, comedian looks uncomfortable) *Yeah... right... I told him that* (laughter starts to die down) *Boy did he look stupid.* (laughter fades) *Isn't that crazy?* (laughter is gone) *I didn't go back there again, that's for sure.* (Comedian looks like a nincompoop)

Veteran comedians always tell beginners, "If you can't say something funny during the laugh, shut up and stand there 'til the audience is done." While this is good advise most amateurs can't put it to use because a roomful of laughing people can be a pretty awkward situation. Good performers, like Burns and Allen, handle laughs by *maintaining their characters* throughout the act, even when laughter prevents them from continuing. That is where the comedy technique of attitude comes in.

Every performer has an attitude. It is what guides them on stage and gives their material direction. Attitude translates into *character*. All performers are a character when they are on stage. Even the typical "guy-next-door" or "gal-you-knew-in-school" comedians are playing some sort of character. Some comedians are easily defined and categorized: Don Rickles is mean and insulting, Richard Pryor is an everyman breaking the rules, Gary Shandling is a confused loser, Pee Wee Herman is a manic, mischievous little boy. Other comedians are less outlandish—Jerry Seinfeld, Mary Tyler Moore, Jack Lemon, Walter Mathau—but even these comedians possess a singular attitude that defines them. Seinfeld is the congenial wise guy with an eye for everyday trivia, Moore is the good-hearted nice girl who just wants to be liked, Lemon is the guy that has all the bad luck of the world dumped on him, and Mathau is the crabby old guy with the soft underside.

Good comedians maintain consistency of character throughout their entire act. Even in silence, a comedians character shines through and continues to project his act for him. Watch a comedian who is telling an angry story about her last trip to Disneyland. When she gets to the punchline about smacking Goofy in the mouth and the audience is laughing, watch how she maintains the angry attitude throughout the laughter. This character trait gives her something to hold onto when she is not able to use words. When she does use words, her character determines how the words are chosen and delivered.

Veteran performers learn to see the world through the eyes of their character. After a while, comedy material seems to flow naturally. This is why many comedians claim that after a number of years on stage they hardly ever plan what to say. Their character is so ingrained that it almost does the talking for them. Most comedians learn to develop characters that are in large part, themselves. That way they don't have to stretch their acting to be believable.

Let's look at a story that demonstrates some of the ideas of premise, set up, and punchline, as well as some comedy writing techniques. This is actually a bit developed by a student in one of my stand-up comedy classes. The first version is the one he told in class, we later tightened it up for use on stage. The first draft contained so many mistakes it broke almost every rule of comedy. After the first draft I'll repeat the story to highlight some of the mistakes. Then we can see how to fix a broken joke.

I've always wanted to be my own boss. I started my own lawn-mowing business because I wanted to be my own boss. You know, be your own boss, set your own hours, no-one hassling you. So I went to a Coast-to-Coast hardware store... or was it Hardware Hank? No, it was Coast-to-Coast. And I got myself a used lawnmower...no...two used lawnmowers 'cause I wanted a partner to help with the mowing and a used lawnmower was cheaper. So I put an ad in the paper for a lawnmowing partner to help me mow the lawns. A guy named Charlie answered the ad and I asked him if he knew what he was doing and he said "Sure." This is a true story. Now when I was at the hardware store I picked up a file just in case the blades on the mower were dull. Well we went to our first job at this ladies house, this is a true story too. We started cutting her grass. Well she was watching us the <u>whole time</u> right from her front window. The blades were kind of dull and they weren't cutting that well so I turned my mower over and started sharpening the blade with the file I got from the hardware store. And the lady's watching us the whole time. Charlie says, "Hey Ray, you don't need to do that. I'll take care of this." And he pulled out a switch blade and started cutting the grass with it. That's a true story.

He got the same reaction from the class as you are giving me right now, a blank stare. Now let's look at the routine and spotlight specific problems.

I started my own lawn-mowing business because I've always wanted to be my own boss.

You know, be your own boss, set your own hours, no-one hassling you.
1. Unnecessary information.

So I went to Coast-to-Coast...or was it Hardware Hank?
2. It doesn't matter which store he went to.

No, it was Coast-to-Coast.
3. Get it right the first time.

And I got myself a used lawnmower, no, two used lawnmowers 'cause I wanted a partner and used was cheaper.

So I put an ad in the paper for a lawnmowing partner to help me mow the lawns.
4. Unnecessary info.

A guy named Charlie answered the ad and I asked him if he knew what he was doing and he said "Sure."
5. By now we've lost interest in the whole story, much less whether he knows lawn care or not.

This is a true story.
6. Auugh!

Now when I was at the hardware store I picked up a file just in case the blades on the mower were dull.
7. Information that doesn't matter, and is being told out of sequence to the order of events.

Well we went to our first job at this lady's house,

this is a true story too,
8. A mistake to say the first time, deadly the second.

and we started cutting her grass.

Well she was watching us the <u>whole time</u> right from her front window.
9. We are lead to believe that the story is about her watching him and that the punchline will relate to her somehow.
The blades were kind of dull and they weren't cutting that well so I turned my mower over and started sharpening the blade with the file I got from the hardware store.
10. Repeat of info.

And the lady's watching us the whole time.
11. We know, we know! We're just waiting for the punchline.

Charlie says, "Hey Ray, you don't need to do that. I'll take care of this." And he pulled out a switch blade and started cutting the grass with it.

12. Punchline not exaggerated enough, no real ending to the story.

That's a true story.

13. Yes, but it's not funny.

Let's look at each point individually.

1. Unnecessary information. You have to assume that the audience at least partially understands what you mean. We all know the benefits of wanting to be your own boss. Too much explanation will destroy humor. The mind is already racing ahead, thinking of all the wonderful comic possibilities, while Ray is stuck on the mundane.

2. Too much detail. This is as bad as when Aunt Flo starts telling us about our *"cousin Milton's bicycle accident when he was 13...or was it 14? No it was 12. I think he was 12. Hey Roger! Was Milton 12 or 13 when he had that bicycle accident?"* You're ready to scream, "Get on with it!" No one really cares about every little detail in a story. People usually include useless details because the story actually happened to them and they think they need to explain *everything* in order for the listener to understand. If a detail is not germane to the plot, leave it out. We listeners instantly soak up the details of a story, knowing that in order to understand the punchline we

will have to pay close attention. If our heads are filled with useless prattle we will quickly lose interest.

3. <u>Get it right the first time.</u> Uncertainty and mix-up of facts causes the listener to lose the suspension of disbelief that allows us to believe the speaker actually lived the story. How can we believe someone lived the story when they can't get simple facts straight. Even if the listener believes the story, it is uninteresting because there is no straight line of thinking. Our reaction is, "This story isn't going anywhere. Why should I pay attention?"

4. <u>Unnecessary information.</u> This can be shortened simply by telling us, "I got a partner to help me."

5. <u>I don't care about the story anymore.</u> Enough said.

6. <u>This is a true story!</u> Never, ever tell the listener it's a true story. We already believe it's true, or want to. We are fully engaged in suspension of disbelief and you ruin the fantasy by reminding us we're listening to a story. Telling us that a story is true only reinforces that fact that you're insecure. I can guarantee that any time a story is followed with, "It really happened," the joke was boring and unfunny so the speaker needed an excuse for telling it to us.

7. <u>Information out of sequence.</u> Tell us the story in the order it happened so we can follow. We don't need to know about the files at this point in the story. Too many facts clutter our brains and cloud the line of thought.

8. <u>True story!</u> Repeating that it's a true story usually means you expected a laugh at this point and didn't get it, so you feel the need to justify telling the story.

9. <u>What's the story about?</u> Keep in mind that the set up of the story is supposed to guide our thoughts in a very direct line to the end. This line makes us think the punchline is related to the lady watching through the window. If the punchline is not about her, don't mention her.

10. <u>Repetition.</u> We already know where the file came from.

11. <u>Again with the repetition!</u> A redundant superfluous overuse of repetitive unnecessary information we shouldn't have initially been told the first time...regardless.

12. <u>Punchline not exaggerated.</u> Although the use of a switchblade to cut grass is unusual, the set up is so long and circuitous that the exaggeration is not strong enough to create surprise and laughter.

13. <u>You're kidding! This is a true story?</u> The whole story bombs, so a last ditch justification is attempted.

The student worked on the story and eventually got it to work with a shortened version, a tighter delivery, and the addition of a tag:

I've always wanted to be my own boss, so I started a lawn mowing service. I got a couple of used lawnmowers and an assistant out of the want-ads. We went to our first job and started mowing. Well, the blades were so dull they weren't cutting so good, so I turned my mower over and started to file the blade down when this guy says, "Hey Ray, don't worry about that. I'll take care of it." And he starts cutting the grass with a scissors. (Ray pauses and looks at his watch) *He's still there.* (Pause during laughter) *What the heck, I got the check.*

Notice how much information is removed from the revised version. We also replaced the harsh, unfunny image of a switchblade with the more humorous *scissors*. Laughter is generated from our ability to visualize the poor assistant still cutting a lawn with a scisors in the middle of the night, and the attitude of superiority of Ray, who took the money and left him there. The revised joke worked very well in performance and Ray was able to use the bit as a call back later in his act. For the call back, it would be much later in his act and he would be talking about how long his old mother takes to do simple tasks. He would describe how frustrating it was to take her to the grocery store because she took forever to select items in the produce section. Ray would say, *"I had to take her to the store again just the afternoon."* he pauses, looks at his watch and says, *"She's still there."* (Pause) *"What the heck, I got the twinkies."*

Let's look at the whole bit again, in detail.

Premise
I've always wanted to be my own boss, so I started a lawn-mowing service.

Set Up
I got a couple of used lawnmowers and an assistant out of the want-ads. We went

223

Set Up

to our first job at a lady's house. Well, the blades were so dull they weren't

Set Up

cutting so good, so I turned my mower over and started to file the blade down when this guy says, "Hey Ray, don't worry about that. I'll take care of it." And

First Punchline

he starts cutting the grass with a scissors. (pauses and looks at his

Punchline

watch) *He's still there.* (Pause during laughter)

Tag

What the heck, I got the check.

(Later in the act)

New Premise

...I can't believe I agreed to take my mom to the grocery store.

Punchline

She takes seven hours to feel one tomato.

Callback/Tag

(pauses and looks at watch) *She's still there."* (Pause)

2nd Callback/2nd Tag

"What the heck, I got the twinkies."

224

Check out the comedy writing techniques in this episode of "The Dick Van Dyke Show." Laura Petrie is talking to her next door neighbor/best friend, Millie Helper. They are talking about the possibility of Laura and her husband Rob staying at Millie and Jerry Helper's cabin for the weekend. Millie has been telling Laura about Jerry's opinions concerning male behavior. The parenthesis describe the type of comedy used.

M: Listen, some husbands will do anything to get out of going away alone with their wives.

L: Well not Rob. Rob and I have been alone together many times.

*M: **Alone**, alone?* (Language, sarcasm)

L: Millie, now stop that! Anyway, where did Jerry learn so much about psychiatry?

M: Well, every morning on the train he plays gin rummy with a psychiatrist. Between Scarsdale and 125th St. a lot soaks in. (Absurdity)

L: Well I think his diagnosis is silly

M: Well why don't you ask Rob if he wants to go and if Jerry's wrong you can have a nice weekend, free.

L: Thank you, I think I will ask him.

(Sound of loud referee's whistle from next door)

M: Oh my gosh, that's Jerry now. He gets so cranky before he's had his breakfast. I'll call you before I leave.

(Unexpected, contrast)

Millie leaves, Rob enters

Rob: Morning honey. What's for breakfast?

L: I got some new cereals. It's the Treasure Chest assortment. You can have Wheatie Wow Wows, Ricey Rumbles, Sesame Sweeties, or Corny Cuties. (List, Absurdity)

R: No Barley Bupkus? (Tag)

L: No. Ritchie ate them. Listen, how about some Corn Flakes?

R: Corn flakes? (Rob laughs) *What a silly name for a cereal. Yeah, I'll have some of them Corn Flakes.*

(Sarcasm)

They begin to discuss plans for the weekend.

L: Well, I thought we could drive up to Lake Sissymenunu.

(Absurdity)

R: Aaaugh!

L: What's the matter?

R: (reaching into cereal bowl) *I almost ate a fire engine.*

(Unexpected contrast)

L: That's a prize, Ritchie's been waiting for this.

R: You want to drive all the way up there for the weekend?

L: Yeah, I'd really love it darling.

R: (reaching in cereal bowl again) *Wait a minute, here's a little ladder.* (Tag)

They begin to discuss going up to the cabin. Rob says that it would be difficult to get away from the office. It is obvious that he doesn't want to go. He finally says that it just wouldn't be fair to his co-workers, Buddy and Sally, for him to leave on such short notice. Laura accuses Rob of creating catastrophes so as not to spend time with her.

R: That just is not true.

L: It is so. Remember the first time you had that cold, and remember the second time you broke out in that mysterious rash.

R: I can't help it if I get sick honey. That's just a coincidence.

L: (in a questioning tone) Was it just a coincidence?

R: (pauses, begins to suspect something is up) *Honey, who've you been talking to?*

L: Millie.

R: And Jerry is the fella that came up with the diagnosis right? (Superiority, being aware of something the character in the story is not)

L: Well all I know Rob, is that you and I never get away alone together anymore.

R: We have been alone three times this year, away.

*L: Not **alone**, alone.*   (Call back)

They finally decide to go to the cabin.

R: It's going to be more than a weekend of fun together. I'm wanna to prove to you once and for all that I want to be alone with you so badly that I'm willing to go up there by myself!

(Absurdity)

The construction of a well-made joke needs as much attention to detail as a presidential speech. Given the

227

importance of the outcome, a comedian's awareness of detail is paramount to success.

Chapter 16
THE CULTURE OF COMEDY

Television is an invention whereby you can be entertained in
your living room by people you wouldn't have in your house.
David Frost

Anyone who watches TV has seen hundreds of stand-up
comedians and comedic actors. The cable network revolution
of the early '90s brought stand-up comedy in particular into a
new era of accessibility. In all it's previous incarnations, stand-
up comedy was a novelty. It was a part of the entertainment
world people thought of as a gypsy-like, almost illegitimate art
form. The '50s stand-up comedian was a good natured clown
thrown in the middle of a variety show for flavor, or between
sets at a rock concert so the next band could set up. In the '60s,
comedy in general, and particularly stand-up, mirrored the
harsh dissatisfied attitude of society. Comedians like Lenny
Bruce and Richard Pryor stretched the boundaries of what
society called good taste. The '70s produced a silly playful
attitude about life, and comedy followed suit with performers
like Steve Martin and shows like The Brady Bunch. The '80s
saw an incredible stand-up boom. Every Holiday Inn and Taco
Bell across America was putting a stage and a microphone in a

lounge or break room for *Stand-Up Showcase Night.* Stand-up became hip. Clubs that only a year earlier were charging $6 per ticket could charge $12-15 plus a two drink minimum (with drinks costing double the normal price). No matter what the content or attitude however, until cable TV, stand-up comedy was a special treat enjoyed as part of an evening out. The late '80s and early '90s, with new 300-seat white table cloth rooms, put stand-up on par with an evening at the theatre, even if the acts weren't quite as high-brow as Shakespeare.

With cable TV came the first all comedy networks, HA! and Comedy Central. Ha! was soon bought by Comedy Central and one comedy network dominated the air. Comedy Central provided the first 24-hour comedy channel, featuring shows ranging from old black-and-white movies to comedy specials, comedy talk shows, sketch troupes, and lots and lots of stand-up. Some shows even featured one stand-up talking to another about...stand-up. Comedy Central wasn't the only TV network to jump on the laugh-wagon. Every major network featured at least one all stand-up comedy show. And the growth of local cable stations in every city allowed anyone to produce and air amateur attempts at funny.

The rampant growth of stand-up was not entirely a good thing. The more comedy programs there are, the more comedians you need. In the '70s and '80s a comedian would have had to work for years to even audition for a spot on TV. The 90's cable wars created such a shortage of talent that almost anyone with access to a third-grade joke book could be seen nationwide. Before the onslaught of cable, a comedian was competing against thousands of other performers for a spot on The Tonight Show, Late-Night with David Letterman, HBO, or Showtime. A spot on any of these shows meant certain success. With cable, the number of shows needing good stand-ups outnumbered the available talent, so a lot of comedians got television exposure who were not nearly ready to make such a huge career leap. Many were given a 10-minute spot simply because they had exactly 10 minutes of good material. Before the cable boom, a 10 minute spot was given to a comedian who had literally hours of material. And that material had stood the test of years of performances in clubs, bars, and bar mitzvahs all over the country.

With so many shows on every night, and the ability to "sweeten" the audience response with canned laughter, the need for highly seasoned comedians diminished. So much stand-up was being pushed on so many channels that the surety of fame through TV exposure vanished—almost every comedian was able to put on their resume "As seen on (insert show here)." In the '70s and '80s, a television appearance instantly jumped a comedians performance fee from $800 per week to $3000 per week. After cable got through diluting the gene pool the only thing comedians could be sure of after a TV appearance was a sweaty shirt from being under the lights. In fact, less experienced comedians actually suffered from premature TV exposure. It displayed their only good material to an entire nation of viewers, leaving them with no new material for club performances.

Comedians themselves also changed. In the pre-'80s era a comedian had to be crazy to pursue a career in stand-up comedy. Long hours at night were spent performing for free at any club that would give you stage time and a microphone. A typical comedian would run home from his day-job, change clothes and hop from club to club 6 nights a week. If he was lucky, after several months or years of honing his craft on every stage from a swanky night club to a VFW hall, he would start to get gigs that paid perhaps $15 a show. A comedian's dream was to someday go "on the road," traveling full-time around the country. The road was where a comedian could make a decent living, ply his craft full-time, and pursue a shot at national TV.

To be good enough for road work a comedian had to have endured a long and stressful period as a novice. And, unlike most jobs where co-workers are understanding and supportive during your training period, beginning comedians rarely receive such support. Other comedians see you as competition for the little work and stage time available. Audiences don't care if you're new or a veteran, if you're not funny they don't like you and they'll make sure you know it. This is not to say that comedians act heinously to each other, on the contrary many form friendships that outlast some marriages. The atmosphere of being a performer, especially a comedic one, can still be wrought with stress.

Before the big boom, success at stand-up was a million-to-one shot and the price for failure was humiliation in front of an audience and the grief of a dream lost. In order to brave those kinds of odds and withstand that kind of pressure a person would need drive and ambition. Comedy would need to go beyond being a love, it would have to be a *need*. As university theatre professors across the country tell their students year, "If you can do anything else but theatre and be happy, do it!" The same applies to comedy. With all these obstacles, a comedian never went into the business for the money.

After the comedy boom hit America, many things changed. Overnight the nation went from a dozen or so comedy clubs sprinkled throughout the country, to hundreds. And fees went up too. Comedians who were making $20 a night were now making $2000 a week. Comedians with no TV credit or national exposure were making $50,000-$75,000 a year on the road. Suddenly everyone wanted to be a comedian for a new reason, money.

When I first designed my college degree—*Theory and Performance of Comedy*—everyone said, "Are you crazy, what kind of a job can you get with that?" When I started teaching improv and stand-up in the early '80s and asked students why they were interested in learning comedy, the reply was always, "It's something I've always dreamed of doing." During the peak of the comedy wave that attitude changed. I would have prospective students ask, "How much money can I make at this?" before they even started class. Suddenly comedy was big business.

What did all this mean for the world of comedy? The result was that stand-up comedy went down the same path of destructive mediocrity that the sit-com did in the '70s. Early sit-coms, the ones developed when TV was still in its infancy, were produced by writers fresh out of the radio era. Radio writers had to possess a keen sense of dialogue and storytelling, since radio relied so heavily on both for entertainment. Comedy of language and character was rich in radio acts like Jack Benny, Abbott and Costello, Burns and Allen, and "The Bickersons." Television programs in the early days were written by writers fresh out of radio. These programs still reflected radios commitment to a tight plot and well crafted characters. As the medium of television matured and more programs began to emerge, producers became wise to the "tricks" of television comedy. They started relying more on a goofy facial expression and visual slapstick for a laugh. As ratings became increasingly more important in order to win advertising sponsors, other elements were mixed into the plot; language that dipped below the belt, with wardrobe to match.

Comedy ceased to break taboos for the purposes of satirical social comment. It instead relied on shock value for laughs and ratings. Shows like "Three's Company," and "Married with Children" were developed, routinely featuring cleavage, prat-falls, and butt jokes. The plot was usually a loose take on a Feydeau Farce or Shakespearean comedy—full of mistaken identities, hidden plots, and failed schemes. Rather than take the classic form of farcical comedy, these shows would instead use the formulas to churn out cookie-cutter copies week after week. When we look at shock comedians like Andrew Dice Clay and the late Sam Kinison, we can see that in some ways man has not progressed much further than the ancient Greeks in our love for obscenity.

An interesting phenomenon occurred with stand-up in the '80s. New groups of people began seeing comedy as a means to express their own life issues. Ethnic and social minorities began to use the stage to affirm their new freedom of expression and individual power. African-Americans, long restricted to the self-deprecating role of "the stupid darkie" in movies and television, were finally gaining respect as accomplished actors and entertainers. Their individual freedoms were gaining footholds after decades of repression. It was their turn to have a say on stage. In delivering their message to the people some chose the path of anger and some chose the path of humor.

When activists like Malcolm X and Louis Farakahn spoke against prejudice and bigotry they helped raise the consciousness of people of all colors, but they also incited hatred, both from those who did not respond well to open criticism and from the choir they were preaching to who were mad as hell and ready to rebel. Up stepped Richard Pryor, Eddie Murphy, George Wallace, Dick Gregory, Bill Cosby, and Sinbad. They were able to convey the same anger and frustration about the same social issues, but with humor as the vehicle, the message was accepted on a much broader scale. Through the derisive power of laughter people began to see the foolishness of racism and bigotry.

A look at Lenny Bruce's routine, "How to Relax your Colored Friends at Parties," shows Bruce's insight about racial tension in the '60s and how much has changed since then. Keep in mind while reading the routine that a good many of

Bruce's friends were black performers, so he was very aware of the hypocritical manner in which many whites supposedly befriended blacks in the '60s. This, coupled with his own unsteady relationship with "normal" society, accounts for the bite in his humor. In this piece, Bruce was selective in his use of offensive language. Each word was used to gain a reaction.

This is the typical white person's concept of how we relax colored people at parties.
(Cocktail music playing in background, Bruce sits down and talks to a black gentleman. Bruce's character is a nasal-voiced smoothie. The party guest is a normal black guy quietly enjoying the evening.) After the initial greetings, Bruce continues the conversation.

Bruce: You're not Jewish are ya? No offense. Some of my best friends are Jews. Had 'em over to the house for dinner. They're all right, uhh you know, some are no good, but ahh...you seem like a white Jew to me. (Uncomfortable pause) *Yeah...that Bojangles, Christ could he tap dance!*

Guy: Yeah.

B: You tap dance a little yourself, eh?

G: Yeah, yeah a little.

B: All you people can tap dance, I guess. You people have a natural sense of rhythm. That's right, born right in ya, I guess, huh? Yeah, the way I figure it is, no matter what the hell a guy is, if he stays in his place he's all right. That's the way I look at it. That's what's causing all the trouble in the world. Everybody uhh ...uhh...well here's to Joe Lewis. Joe

Lewis was a guy who ...the way I figure, he was guy who just knew when to get in there and get outta there. That's more than I can say for a lot of you niggers. No offense, I had a few (drinks) on the way over here. You're all right, you're...you're a good boy. Ah...did you have anything to eat yet?

G: No, I haven't. I'm quite hungry too.

B: Well, if there's any watermelon left, ah...fried chicken...we'll see if we can fix   you up with something.

Lenny Bruce

The Best of Lenny Bruce

Bruce's pull-no-punches approach to comedy often insulted those who saw themselves as "above" the behavior he described. In some cases, his directness landed him in jail on charges of public obscenity. Many comedians today have found ways to get their message across in gentler means, but there are still many who relish the harsher in-your-face style of Bruce. His pointed humor can still be found in many of the on-edge clubs around the country.

The manner in which blacks grew in prominence in mainstream comedy illustrates a pattern common to many groups. Each new group that achieves power in our society expresses themselves through comedy, and each group follows the same progression of comedic maturity. After african-americans established their presence with all black comedies—"Good Times," "The Jeffersons," "What's Happening?," "In Living Color," "Martin," and "Def Comedy Jam,"—other groups began to seek recognition. Before the popularity of stand-up, professional comediennes could be counted on one hand. Pioneers such as Lucille Ball, Lily Tomlin, Joan Rivers, and Phyllis Diller were the exception, not the rule. In the '80s women took stand-up and sit-com by storm with "Rosie O'Donnell's Stand-Up Spotlight," "SHE TV," "Ladies of the Night," "It's a Living," "Golden Girls," and "Designing Women." In 1995, latin-american humor was featured on nationwide TV with the comedy variety show, "House of Buggin'" featuring John Luguisamo. The first asian-american woman to reach stand-up prominence was Margaret Cho, following in the footsteps of 80's star, Johnny Yun.

Just as a new comedian resorts to low comedy and juvenile material until his experience allows him to expand to more substantial subject-matter, groups of new performers often follow the same pattern. Blended with the pattern of comedic maturity is a pattern of establishing control in the new arena of comedy. When blacks first started gaining prominence in comedy, most of the humor revolved around sex jokes and foul language. Richard Pryor's early routines focused largely on low comedy shock value. Mixed in with the sexual material was a good deal of humor directed at the stupidity of whites, sometimes combining the two themes with bits about sex with white women. As his career progressed and his stature as a comedian grew his humor became more broad based. He began illuminating inadequacies of all people, regardless of race—often turning the comic light on himself. Some would say that this was a reaction of the social climate—that Pryor at first reacted to the '60s atmosphere of racial tension and redefining ethnic boundaries and later followed the '70s attitude of silliness with movies like, "Silver Streak," and "Stir Crazy." However, Pryor was doing more than following the attitude of the country, he was following a path all comedians walk, that of personal *comedic maturity*.

All groups follow the same pattern of comedic maturity, no matter the era. Each group first establishes its identity to the general audience with an "us against them" mentality. Jokes are usually inside observations about how "we" are different from "them." This unites the group. It defines their identity and bonds the performer with the audience. This is especially important since, in the beginning, the comedian is most likely playing to an audience made up of his or her own culture. When the group begins to gain social power the need for circling the wagons is not as strong, and other areas of humor can be explored. The group feels comfortable including itself as the brunt of the joke and begins to use humor to actually break down the same social walls that humor had previously been used to build.

When women first broke into stand-up *en mass* in the '80s the predominant focus of their material was feminine hygiene products, child-birth, PMS., dating, and men (specifically, what women hated about men). Jokes about intimate subjects like menstruation and personal hygiene rely mainly on shock value on the part of the male audience, recognition on the part of women, and embarrassment on the part of everybody. These were the most easily recognizable subjects that separated women from men and established a niche for women in comedy. In order to gain acceptance from your own peers, and thereby gain a friendly ear from the audience, you must first establish common ground. Women's dealings with men are a sure way to garner support from women in the audience. Once firm ground is established the comedian is able to venture into broader material.

As time went by, more and more women were given support in the field of comedy and the scope of their humor broadened. Lily Tomlin accomplished this in *The Search for Intelligent Life in the Universe.* This one-woman show took comedy far beyond what most women were attempting at the time, and opened up the field for a host of mono-woman shows to follow.

As each subculture gains social power, humor *towards* that group also changes. As the decades progressed and new groups gained social power, jokes about blacks, Jews, women, and gays became more and more unacceptable on stage and off. In the past, groups of people would deride other groups to reaffirm their own status. As each group came to comedy prominence and society became more educated, it became inappropriate to continually make those groups a target of ridicule. In many ways, humor helped erase insensitivity by providing a safe means of educating the public. The result for comedy was twofold, people were maturing in their use of humor, and the old target groups were not taking ridicule lying down. Perhaps it is not so fun to pick on an enemy who can either fight back as good as you, or will make you feel like a louse for even opening your mouth. In a time of being politically correct, a loud-mouthed, bigoted clown is no longer considered funny, unless he is being used to make fun of other loud-mouthed, bigoted clowns.

Comedians are in a constant search for acceptable targets for humor. Given that they must appeal to the broadest audience possible, it is difficult to know where the line of good taste is drawn. It is no wonder that many comedic performers circumvent the whole mess by making *themselves* the brunt of the joke. If you are constantly making yourself look like the fool, no one will question your good taste—and you are more often forgiven if every now and then you take a stab at someone else.

In the culture of comedy, the most exciting promise is that there is always a new group or subculture ready to take the stage and show us a new approach to humor.

Chapter 17
WHAT ARE THEY LAUGHING AT OVER THERE?

"Men show their character in nothing
more clearly than by what they think laughable"
Goethe

Laughter is the most universal expression in the world (next to a handshake or a punch in the nose). It is also true that most people laugh at the same things. The steps of Stevie Ray's Pyramid of Comedy apply to all laughter, no matter what the source or cultural backdrop. The pyramid can describe laughter in any language or country, but there are cultural differences that affect the subject matter of comedy.

Many factors determine the object of laughter in a culture. The most important of which is, who is in control. Those in control will always be the target of jokes by those with no power. The level of education, as well as the social and economic conditions of society also play a large part in the forming of that society's sense of humor. Laughter is an important part of every culture and the manner in which it is regulated reflects the core of that cultures philosophy. For even though we all find humor in the same things, the rules of our society don't allow us to equally express our appreciation of humor. A stuffy nobleman from Europe may have been raised in such a strict proper environment that, even though he finds a man falling on his butt hilarious, he would never allow himself the freedom to laugh at the man. Eventually this repression can change the individual's opinions of what is and is not funny. Societies have social priorities which affect its members' comedic understanding. An agricultural community may not be well-read enough to understand humor of a literary nature. Students at Yale may not understand why farmers laugh at bovine jokes.

Some societies place immense importance on the simple act of laughter. In the Navajo Indian culture children are seen as a precious gift to the tribe. To ensure that a newborn child is constantly watched and cared for, Navajo tradition dictates that the baby be kept in a cradle board until the child laughs for the first time. Whomever makes the baby laugh must arrange for a celebration in honor of the child. This celebration is called the First Laugh ceremony. It is at this time that the child is fully accepted as a member of the tribe. The Navajo believe laughter marks the child's birth as a social being. Before then, the child is no different than an animal because it has not engaged in the one act besides speech that separates humans from animals, laughter. The Navaho are also correct in that laughter is the first truly social act a person engages in. All actions before then are centered on the self and stem from the need to survive. Clasping to the mother for protection, taking milk for nourishment, sleeping, crying, and waiting for the diapers to be changed are all acts of selfish need. Laughter is the first step to realizing human interaction and appreciating family, friends, and tribe.

Seeing how comedy is enjoyed in other countries can help us better understand our own sense of humor. Obviously it is neither possible nor practical to fully examine every country's style of humor, so I have taken what I think are interesting examples of humor from a few countries and offered explanations as to their origin. If you happen to be from any of these countries, please don't write to me with, "but our humor is so much broader than you give us credit." I know, I know. Write your own book.

Russia

Citizens of the former Soviet Union were not afforded a fraction of the freedom that Americans enjoy. So it stands to reason that their humor would reflect their oppressed state. One can see surface effects of a communist regime in the fact that entertainers had to censure every word they said on stage, lest it offended the powers that be. The famous Russian immigrant comedian, Yakov Smirnov, was amazed at the freedom performers are given in the US In Smirnov's homeland, every single joke in a comedian's act had to be approved by a government bureau. In America we protest the slightest raise in taxes, especially if the proposed program seems frivolous to us. Imagine what American citizens would do if they learned that their hard earned taxes were going to pay for a Bureau of Joke Approval. The air of oppression in the USSR naturally gave Russian humor a bit of a soft edge on stage, and a biting one in private.

Communism has strong effects on the very psyche of its people. It creates an atmosphere that is better reflected in the jokes told by everyday folks on the street than by the professional on stage or screen. These jokes illuminate the problems of day to day life in such a culture.

A man in Russia had problems with his sink, so he called a state plumber.

After hearing the problem the plumber said, "I'll be able to fix it in ten years."

The man asked, "In ten years will you be coming in the morning or the afternoon?"

The plumber asked, "Why?"

The man said, "Because I have an electrician coming in the morning."

Imagine the punishment that would await the comedian who delivered such a joke on Russian television. This joke—popular in the USSR, but told only among friends—does what every good joke should do, it speaks about what is foremost on the peoples minds. A visit to Russia or neighboring countries of the former USSR quickly displays what years of communism have wrought on the population. The black market is almost the only way to secure the simple goods that most of us find available in stores everywhere. Alcoholism is so rampant that vodka has actually become a form of currency on the black market. It is used as a bartering tool for everything—food, supplies, gasoline, clothing, and electronics. The phrase, "How many bottles does it cost?" is common. It is not surprising to learn that many jokes in Russia center around alcohol.

Three men in were stranded in a lifeboat. They discover to their dismay that there is only one bottle of vodka. Since one bottle is obviously too little to share, they decide that the man who could tell the wildest, most unbelievable story could have the bottle. The first man began and told a tale of a large fish overturning the boat, and all three men being swallowed and carried in the fish for days until the fish got caught in a fishing net and the three men were rescued. At the end of the story the other two were slightly impressed, but said that the story could probably happen, so it was not creative enough. The second man told an equally wild story of storms rocking the boat, shirts and pants used for sails, and rescue by mermaids of the sea. The other two men were impressed, but it was still not good enough. Finally, the third man began. He told a story of three men who set out on a boat ride, saying good-bye to their friends and family, asking them not to drink the 100 bottles of vodka they had left on the beach for a welcome home party. They sailed for three days and caught many fish and returned to find that the village had dutifully waited for their return and the whole town opened the 100 bottles of vodka and celebrated together. At the end of this story the two men agreed that this was the most unbelievable story yet. They gave him the bottle, saying that no village would let 100 bottles of vodka sit for three days unopened.

This story demonstrates that the Russian people are not only aware of their over-love of alcohol, but they are comfortable enough to joke about it. It is also a telling thing that in the story it is automatically assumed that one bottle of vodka isn't enough to share between three men in a boat. This is indeed a sad statement on the degree of alcohol consumption present in Russia.

Russia prides itself on tradition. When a society has very little by way of material goods, it looks to other sources for self-esteem. In America we envy the man or woman with a big house and nice car, in Russia those things aren't even an option for most common people. So the Russians turn to less tangible sources of pride; family, political and military heroes, and religion. Knowing what is important to a society allows us to satirize those things.

A man once said to his woman, "Ever since the baby was born all you talk about is marriage."

In America, with its more flexible views on marriage and relationships, this joke gets a mild chuckle, in Russia it gets guffaws. This demonstrates that the more oppressive a policy or ideology is, the more it will be satirized. Humor is the only way people can really feel a sense of personal power and freedom in the face of oppression.

Another fact about Russia demonstrates the theory of *comedic maturity* at the social level. People find physical humor more funny as a young person, while later in life they tend to like more intellectual comedy. Russia, as a whole, enjoys physical humor much more into adulthood. My brother Richard was managing a worksite in the Ukraine when a laborer fell off a ladder and onto his backside. An event like this in America would elicit a giggle or two from the gang, then everyone would get back to work. The entire Ukraine crew laughed for fifteen minutes solid—they actually had tears rolling down their cheeks. They acted as if it was the funniest thing they had ever seen and they talked about the incident for days, laughing still every time the incident was retold.

Humor is often used to expose inequities in society, this is true in Russia as well. If a Russian man is too stupid to get a good job he can always be hired as a policeman. This is truly ironic, since the last person you would want ensuring public safety is the town fool. As such, police jokes are also common.

How does a policeman check to see how many matches are left in a box? (Action of the policeman holding the box up to his ear and shaking his head instead of the box.)

Now that the USSR is no more, with trade and commerce increasing with the US, it will be interesting to see how humor changes. Politicians and other people in power will always remain the brunt of humorous attacks, but everyday life jokes may take on a different flair.

Japan

Japan is a nation built on etiquette, tradition, loyalty, family, and social status. It is a nation of contradictions. Japan can produce some of the most advanced technology in the world, yet its educational system all but squelches independent thought. It is one of the most industrious of modern societies, yet alcoholism is rampant among adult males because going to bars and drinking is considered as much a part of the job as working. It is a culture steeped in personal honor, yet it is common for married men to have a mistress. The contradictions are obvious and confusing to everyone...except the Japanese. A close look at the workings of this complex society can explain why the Japanese think and react the way they do, and can also explain their particular approach to humor.

While visiting Japan in 1982 I was surprised to discover that, although their society is much different than that of Russia, their appreciation of humor is very similar. In everyday conversation I was always sure to get a laugh if I included wild gestures and facial expressions. Acting silly in this manner in America would be perceived as "pushing too hard for a laugh." We would actually resist laughing if we saw someone acting too silly. In Japan however, it was greeted with delight—both children and adults giggled and laughed freely. In fact, I noticed that the majority of people I came to know gave themselves the freedom to act much more child-like than the typical American. A sixteen-year-old girl giving me a tour of a high school went skipping down the hall like a six-year-old. In America this would be met with jeers and insults from classmates, but in Japan it didn't raise an eyebrow. On the last day of my visit I gave the father my host family a few bottles of fine American whiskey. While such a gift in America would generate a smile and a warm "thank you," the Japanese gentleman leaned back in his chair, kicked his feet up in the air, and giggled wildly. He kept repeating, "I am so lucky! I am so lucky! I am so lucky!" At one point he took the bottles and cradled them in his arms saying, "Mine, mine, mine, all mine."

This is not to say that all Japanese humor is low comedy and the nation is filled with comedic children. One must realize that, when a language barrier exists between cultures, most forms of communication must involve larger movements and exaggerated facial expressions just to make one's self understood. This is bound to carry over into humor as well, but I noticed a difference in the very manner of the Japanese that showed that this style of comedy had a strong base in their humor. Indeed, the movies produced in Japan are known for having larger-than-life characters and very physical plots.

The fact that Japanese men will stay out at bars until late every night demonstrates that a society that works hard must also play hard. And people who spend their days taxing their brains don't need comedy that does the same. Many forms of

Japanese entertainment mirror their culture of dignity, inner reflection, and the honoring of ancestors. The very ancient and honored *Noh* and *Kibuki* theatre styles contain precise choreography, costumes, and characters depicting classic tales and important historical events. The Kodo Drummers travel the world performing age-old Japanese musical instruments. And the Japanese Tea Ceremony, perhaps the most exacting ritual in Japan, dictates etiquette and style using formal tenets of behavior dating back centuries. Other pastimes, however, demonstrate that the Japanese people *love to party*. Festivals and celebrations have been known to last for days, with participants drinking and singing until they virtually pass out from exhaustion. It would seem that to live in a pressure-cooker society such as this means that the safety valve must be set to burst occasionally for everyone to let off steam.

The Japanese have a philosophy about letting go of the reins of etiquette. You may have met some traveling Japanese and wondered why they acted with such reckless abandon, doing things that they would never do at home—visiting strip bars, having wild parties, acting out in public places. There is a saying in Japan, "When you're on a trip, throw away your shame." When Japanese are engaged in everyday life at home they are under constant scrutiny from family, friends, co-workers, and society in general. In fact, if a Japanese child acts inappropriately in public, any adult that witnesses the offending behavior may take the child by the hand up to the parent and berate the parent for not acting responsibly to control the child. In America this would be met with, "Take your hands off my kid. I'll raise him however I want!" In Japan, the "incompetent parent" apologizes and vows to correct the mistake. In another example of public watchfulness, a friend and I were waiting to cross a street in downtown Tokyo. Being good Americans, we didn't wait for the light to signal WALK, we saw that there was no cross traffic and all the other cars were waiting for the light to change. With no oncoming cars in sight we dashed across the street against the light. Every car in sight flashed their lights and honked their horns in disapproval. We later observed that, even when no traffic is present, crowds of Japanese will wait until the light signals WALK before moving. This kind of public attention to the individual has given the Japanese an incredibly low crime rate per capita and a society where thousands of yen can be mistakenly forgotten on a subway and every bit is returned to the owner. In fact, a Japanese businessman was leaving a bank in Osaka when a huge gust of wind blew his attaché case from his arms, bursting it open and scattering tens of thousands of yen into the wind. Instantly every Japanese passerby dropped what they were doing and scattered to retrieve the money. All but about 50 yen were retrieved, those were blown too far to catch. You can well imagine what the result would have been had that scenario happened in New York or Chicago.

The downside of this kind of public scrutiny is of course, a very stressful life, feeling like your every action is under a microscope can be unnerving. Many Americans need to sit on the psychiatrists couch for years just to get over an overbearing father. Imagine having an overbearing country! Traveling to other countries affords the Japanese the opportunity to really let go with no one watching and judging them. Comedy in Japanese society becomes an integral part of survival. And since a festival only comes along a few times a year, it is necessary to make a comic attitude a part of everyday life.

An indication of the Japanese everyday comic attitude is the people's willingness to improvise in social situations. On a bus tour in Japan the tour guide may, without notice, pass the microphone from passenger to passenger. Each person takes turns singing a song, reciting a poem, or telling a joke. In school students may be asked to give an impromptu speech. In America this would be met with sullen resistance, in Japan the child jumps up and starts talking. A society that pushes hard for etiquette and control needs to allow occasional abandon in order to preserve sanity.

On a tangential note, the importance of being aware of cultural differences in communication was made clear to me when I was playing with some young Japanese children in a park. I was teasing them with the old, "Got your nose!" game we play with our own kids in America. It is a silly game where you pretend to grab their nose between your thumb and forefinger, slip it off and show them that you've "Got their nose" by closing your hand and sticking your thumb between the first two fingers. As you wiggle your thumb it looks like the tip of their nose poking through. I was having fun with three or four children. Even though I couldn't speak Japanese I assumed they knew what I was doing. Like every American I figured they would understand me if I just spoke slowly and loudly. As soon as the parents saw what I was doing they grabbed their children and hurried away, giving me looks of shock and anger. I had no idea why they were offended. I thought perhaps strangers weren't supposed to play with other people's children. A Japanese friend of mine saw this and quickly took me aside, explaining that the gesture I was making to the children was the Japanese version of "giving the finger." I had no opportunity to find the parents of the children I "flipped off" and explain my mistake. To this day they think there was a rude American running up to their children making obscene gestures. I left the country very soon afterward.

Japanese humor has a strong basis in word play and puns. The sounds of words and the differences in dialect are a good source of Japanese laughter. In the following joke one should understand that the basis of the punchline is the fact that the word "Chu" in Japan means both "mouse" and "middle" (as in large, *medium*, small, or upper, *middle*, lower).

A Japanese man said to a friend, "Yesterday I caught a very large mouse." His friend said, "Oh, I bet it was only a small mouse." The man said, "No, it was a very large mouse." The mouse finally spoke up and said, "Chu!"

Sounds play a large part of Japanese humor because the Japanese language has only 50 sounds (compared to the over 100 sounds in English). As in all countries, differences in dialect are a source of ridicule and humor. The northern Japanese of Tokyo delight in hearing the difference between their speech and those in the southern city of Osaka. We Americans hear no difference whatsoever, they all sound like actors in a Godzilla movie, but they can hear distinct differences. And, as in all ethnic and regional humor (Laughter of Superiority in Chapter 11), those from the agricultural region of Japan have the "southern" dialect and are seen as less sophisticated. Those from the north are seen as snooty and pretentious.

One major factor in the creation of dialect, besides education and social status, is climate. Hotter climates produce slower speech—the southern drawl. This allows heat to escape the body through the mouth. Hot weather also causes a person to physically slow down in order not to overheat the body. Colder climates have the opposite effect. People in Maine and Canada have clipped speech because their mouths must stay shut to preserve heat. You can look worldwide and find that, no matter what the technique of the language is, a hotter climate will create a dialect that is more open-mouthed and slower than a cold climate dialect.

Japan has a southern dialect that is slower and more languid than that of the north. The difference in dialect is clear to the native Japanese. The Japanese say that their southerners have such a strong accent that they are almost unintelligible to northerners, and vice versa. I just can't understand anyone over there.

It will be fascinating to witness changes in Japanese humor as our two cultures continue to blend. The Japanese philosophy has always been to adopt the culture of any nation that conquers it. In this way they attempt to achieve ultimate victory, conquering by assimilation. Before contact with China, Japanese religion was based primarily on Shinto, a belief that honors nature and ancestors. After the invasion of the Mongols in 1274 and 1281 Chinese Buddhism began to make its way into Japanese religion. The Japanese believe that if a country is able to conquer it, that country must have systems and beliefs that are superior, and therefor should be adopted. Christianity was introduced by St. Francis Xavier in the 16th century, but did not take hold until well after the end of World War II when America demonstrated its superiority in war. This attention to social status is evident in every aspect of Japanese culture. Your status as compared to others in a room dictate your every behavior–where you sit at a dinner table, who bows lower and longer in greeting, who soaks first in the hot tub, who makes direct eye contact, and who has final word in debate.

The Japanese have a remarkable capability to accept other ideas into their own culture without conflict. Most western religions have an "us versus them" mentality, whereas many Japanese consider themselves Buddhists, Shinto, and Christians at the same time with no conflict.

It wasn't until first contact with China in the Taika Period (645-710 a.d.) that Japan formed it's first centralized government, using China as a model. This ability to accept other ideas without perceiving them as a threat will no doubt affect the Japanese style of humor, and the manner in which it is performed.

A funny story about assimilation happened when I visited a high school in Japan. In their haste to acquire anything from America, Japanese students will buy US t-shirts by the dozen. One such student walked proudly into class wearing a black t-shirt with huge white letters that said F--K! (edit mine, the shirt didn't edit a thing). The student had no idea what he was wearing as he made his way toward his ENGLISH class. I told a Japanese friend who caught him just in time.

If America has one industry that out-performs any other nation, it is entertainment. Japan is already in love with our movies and music. With a culture that absorbs outside ideas so readily it won't be long before Japanese comedy will include much of our own techniques. I wish I could learn the language, I could have some great overseas comedy gigs.

France

Jerry Lewis is their national hero. What else do you need to know?

England

What is this strange country that could gave us both
Shakespeare and Benny Hill? A quick viewing of British
television shows that this is a truly schizophrenic nation. They
can't seem to decide between kick-in-the-bum slapstick and
witty repartee. Actually, all cultures enjoy each of the seven
levels of the pyramid of comedy. Humor from England and
Great Britain has long had the stereotype of being very heady
and pompous. It is true that Americans enjoy humor that is
character or situation-based and the Europeans are in general
more language oriented. However it is also true that Brits show
a definite love for Low Comedy. Besides Benny Hill's fart-
loving, girl-chasing, naughty-limericking, scatological brand of
humor, there are shows with wacky storylines and goofy
characters. The sit-com, "Faulty Towers" is a wonderful
example. The shows star, John Cleese, makes use of every
prat-fall imaginable. And the plot twists would make
Shakespeare proud. Other shows, "The Neighbors," "Monty
Python's Flying Circus," and the radio adaptation of "The
Hitchhiker's Guide to the Galaxy," demonstrate that the
English taste for comedy closely mirrors our own. As you
recall in Chapter 8, the English love of language has the

members of the House of Lords fighting for victory in nothing but a test of verbal wit.

The laws of comedy are the same for all people, regardless of what country they call home. Feelings of superiority, recognition, surprise, and the urge to reward or reprimand the behavior of those around us are universal. The challenges of everyday life are really no different for an Australian bush tribe than for a family living in an upscale suburban home. We all need to make a living, we all need to feed the kids. The economy will be heavy on our minds whether we trade in dollars or goat-skins. We will probably never lose the tendency to question our leaders, so we will forever make jokes about them whether it's the president, the parliament, or the witch doctor. Where-ever there is a caste-like society there will be jokes about "the other people," where-ever there is inequity there will be satire. Where-ever there are people living together there will be the need to bond with laughter.

Part IV
WHAT NOW?

Chapter 18
BE FUNNIER

This chapter is the real reason why many of you picked up the book in the first place. Most people I meet would love to increase their chances at getting laughs either in front of a business group, a bunch of friends, or when sitting down to dinner with a blind date from the personal ads. I wish I could say that the simple act of reading this book would do the trick, but that ain't so. I can say that now because you've already paid for it, unless you're one of those who stand in the book store reading the good parts.

The first step to accessing your humor is to realize where true humor comes from. When you look at the Levels of Comedy, and the Conditions and Laws of Laughter, you see that to create laughter the comedian must step outside of the boundaries of society. This doesn't mean that you have to be a wild person acting crazy and making a joke out of every word your friends say, but you do have to be the one to break the rules a little. As you can see from watching professional comedians, how far you break the rules depends on your personal sense of humor and how you approach comedy.

You have to take a good objective look at your personality and see how it fits with the Conditions, Laws, and Techniques of comedy we've discussed so far. Comedy needs certain conditions to exist. If you're not willing to provide those elements you will not be a funny person. To provide those necessary components and create laughter you have to be willing to take a risk. It's easy to allow others to take the risk of making funny. If their jokes are funny everybody has a good laugh, if not, well you didn't have to open your mouth and look like the fool so you're comfortable. If you're willing to take the risk there are simple things to practice to get you started.

To take the edge off the risk of being funny remember this, everyone loves a person with good humor. I say *good humor* instead of a good *sense* of humor because there's a difference between the two. A good sense of humor is what everyone wants from a mate, which really translates into "I want someone with *my* sense of humor." We think someone's funny not because they laugh, but because they laugh at the same things we laugh at. Good humor is not laughing all the time, but having the spirit of humor. Being able to see the world, not as a perpetual joke (those people are annoying), but as a place for good feelings between people. Even sarcastic humor, because it's done for the sake of fun, gives people good feelings. If you can take charge of creating good humor, then laughter is the by-product. In this way, you don't have to work at getting laughs, they come as a result of your attitude.

As you look at your personality you should examine how you interact with people. How you approach simple interaction will tell you if you support the rules and techniques of comedy. You could unconsciously be breaking all the rules. Now that you know the elements of comedy, you can see where you might be stepping on the one condition that is needed for humor. Remember, the conditions and laws of laughter don't apply only to the stage, they are necessary for laughter to occur anywhere.

Don't be funny

This is perhaps the most common mistake people make when trying to become a funnier person. We all someone who tries too hard to be funny, cracking jokes all the time and pushing for a laugh where-ever possible. These people are annoying! Don't become one of them because you've decided that humor is your new goal. I explained earlier in the book that people don't like the feeling of being controlled. They like to be offered humor, not have it pushed on them. Humans have a way of resisting when pushed. The same is true for drama. Remember the last cheesy old movie you saw where the acting was stiff and pushy? Even though the movie was supposed to be dramatic you couldn't help but laugh at how bad the acting was. Very poor drama illicits laughter, very poor comedy illicits groans.

If you appear to be trying for a laugh you will meet resistance. You will also look pathetic. It's like when you were a kid hanging out with your friends. If a younger kid wanted to hang out with you it was annoying because he could never keep up with the conversation. If you offer your humor with the eagerness that you hope it gets a laugh you will look like a little kid trying to fit in with an older gang. Instead, offer a strong personality. People will be attracted to you personally and your humor will better take hold.

Lighten up

A *light-hearted atmosphere* and *permission to laugh*. If you are to be the one creating laughter you are responsible for making sure these conditions exist. If they aren't in place, you may be able to create them. If the atmosphere isn't right, don't try. People laugh because they feel relaxed and happy. When you go to a comedy club and the comedian on stage is confident and in control you feel you can relax because he or she is taking care of you. You know you can sit back and not worry about the evening. The confidence of the performer not only lightens the atmosphere, but also gives you permission to laugh. Indeed, many comedians are so powerful that the audience laughs because the delivery is such that they know when they *should* laugh. This goes beyond permission and into guiding the audience to a laugh. If the comedian hit shaky ground and told some jokes that weren't funny, the audience would still be okay, because they know that the performer is still in charge. They trust that things will get back to funny soon.

<u>"Be confident, stupid!"</u>

Problems in comedy occur when the comedian is not confident and in control. When we in the audience see a comedian failing and getting nervous and flustered, we are no longer relaxed. We start to empathize with the poor guy. We put ourselves in his place and think, "Man, am I glad that's not me up there." There is no way a nice audience would laugh at the expense of a dying comedian. This may sound odd for those of you who have been to comedy clubs and seen hostile audiences. The truth is, while there may be a few drunk hecklers in the crowd, very few people laugh at a comedian's failure. There's nothing funny about it. The audience is there to laugh, not feel sorry for someone. By showing nervousness the comedian has demonstrated that he is not in control. In one step the comedian has removed the light-hearted atmosphere and the permission to laugh.

A big step to being funnier is to recognize this important aspect of laughter and utilize it. If you want to make people laugh, you must be confident. No matter what the situation, you must show that your are comfortable and in control. This applies to the stage, the board room, or the dinner table. No one likes to give a pity laugh to someone who gave a lame attempt at humor and then looked like a hurt puppy. Now is the time to pay attention to every time you try humor. If people laugh, fine. If not, examine your attitude and delivery. Did you say your ideas with guts, or did you back down a little at the end, shrug your shoulders, shake your head, or weaken your voice? Any little sign of self-doubt will destroy the audiences ability to laugh. Show them you are in control. If an attempt at humor fails, show everyone you are okay with it. They will trust you, follow you, and forgive the occasional pitfall.

Have a target

If you are afraid of offending people, don't try to be funny. As we see from Laughter of Superiority, people need to feel they are besting someone in order to laugh. If there is no target, there is no laughter. The problem for most people when dealing with humor is finding the right balance. Some people make **everything** a target. They risk looking insensitive and vulgar. Others are so middle of the road they don't really say anything definitive. Comedy is about taking a stance and saying, "To hell with what *you* think. This is what *I* think." If your opinion doesn't have a target, then you are just having pleasant conversation.

Comedians talk about what is stupid in the world, what is odd, what is wrong, what is right, what is unfair, what costs too much, what takes too long, what they don't get, what they do get. They never just talk about what *is*. What *is* is boring. What *should be* is funny.

Opinions, Feelings, and Attitude

Where do you get good comedy material? YOUR LIFE. You already have the only prerequisite a comedian needs, an opinion. The only difference between you and a comedian is that comedians *speak* their opinions. As far as fodder for material, the same is true for on stage and off. Talk about what you know. Talk about what you live. We humans have an amazing capacity for thinking that our wonderful rich lives are boring and that no one would be interested in us. We all live very entertaining lives (if you're a mail carrier in Burke, South Dakota, disregard this). All you have to do is present your predicaments, failures, successes, and quirks to the world. Believe me, people love to listen about other peoples lives. That's why they tune in to Oprah, Sally, Montel, and Maury.

Your life is interesting if you act like it is. Have a strong opinion about things. Act as if your opinion were fact. Good comedians never say, "I think...," they say, "This is..." If you're ever stuck for what to say, think of things you hate, things you love, things that confuse you, things that turn you on, that turn you off. If you live it, and talk about it with passion, people will listen. The more passion you give, the funnier it is. A large part of comedy is *attaching importance to trivia,* and nothing seems more trivial than someone ranting about a problem that is insignificant in our eyes.

Break the rules

As I said earlier, comedy is a risk. Comedians break the rules. Some in big obnoxious ways, some in subtle ways. A rule you break may be as simple as noticing something stupid and instead of thinking, "Well I'm sure there's a reason for that. And it would be impolite to say anything" you say, "Hey. That's stupid!" One of the most common reactions to a funny person is other people saying, "I can't believe she said that!" You are breaking one of society's "be polite" rules. You don't have to be an obnoxious pig about it, but you do have to step forward and say what's on your mind. A comedians greatest compliment besides laughter is someone saying, "I wish I had said that." In order to reap that reward you have to step forward and risk hearing, "That was a stupid thing to say." So realize that the world isn't going to come crashing down if you stick your foot in your mouth once in a while. Take a chance and say something outlandish.

Break routine

In order for laughter to occur there must be a surprise. Daily routine kills laughter, no surprises. I know a prominent neurosurgeon who, whenever he passes the nurses station, does something goofy. Sometimes he tap dances, sometimes he sings a little ditty (what's the difference between a ditty and a song?). He always gets a laugh because he's so different than the other employees of the clinic. Of course, he give himself a challenge because the nurses know to expect something goofy, so each goofy has to exceed each previous goofy. It's the best challenge of the day and one he looks forward to with delight.

If you have a daily routine, simply breaking it with a fun alternative will create laughter. Instead of answering the phone with the same old "Hi, may I help you?" Try to *lighten the atmosphere*. I hear from some business people that one must maintain a business-like demeanor at work. Thppppbt! I deal with Fortune 500 companies all the time and the reason they like dealing with me is that I stick out from the crowd. I certainly don't act obnoxious and weird, but I have fun. And my having fun gives them permission to have fun. And it's no big trick to throw in a little fun. Someone asks me the fees for a corporate workshop and I'll say, "Well it's usually $950,000, but for you HALF PRICE!" It's not a wacky comedy routine, but it's fun and it lightens up the atmosphere and it tells my client *it's okay to laugh.*

People who are afraid to be individuals will always be considered a part of the flock of sheep. If you stand out with a strong attitude and a humorous demeanor it shows you are in control. Only someone who is truly comfortable and confident attempts humor. And it doesn't matter what role you play. I talked to someone recently at the Minnesota Department of Revenue, and he was FUNNY. Moreover, he was fun.

"And a gooood morning to you. Department of Revenue."

"Yeah, I need to order a replacement tax form."

"Well don't worry. We won't hold that against you. What company is this for?"

"Stevie Ray's"

"I think I've heard of you guys. Were you on America's Most Wanted?"

We went on to conduct business in about the same amount of time as it would normally take, but it was a hoot. He decided long ago he could either be a drone in the system and retire all dried up, or he could have fun every day and love going to work. You can't have fun unless you make it a priority. If you don't, the little things that have to get done during the day will take over your brain and you'll end up looking like one of those robots who work at the department of motor vehicles.

One bank president I worked with had learned the lesson of comedy. While in his office working on some papers, we mis-wrote some information on one sheet. He crumpled it up, stood up, and drop-kicked it to the waste basket. When he missed, he retrieved the paper ball and kept kicking until he hit the basket. These aren't wild and crazy things, but they are enough to infuse a comedy spirit in you that will affect how you approach every interaction. Try something a little crazy, then work your way up. Your comfort zone will increase every time.

You can see that breaking the rules is not really all that dangerous. We're not talking about hijacking an airliner to get a laugh, but some people are so afraid of sticking out of the crowd that they squelch their comedic potential. Sticking out of the crowd with something as powerful as humor is essential to success. Look at your everyday life and see what routines you can break. How can you stick out a little and create some healthy laughter.

Practice, practice...

The final word on being funnier is the advise you get when learning any new skill...practice. It seems like an odd thing to actually try practicing. Are you supposed to stand in front of a mirror and make wacky faces at yourself? That wouldn't hurt, but there are things you can do to make humor a more regular part of your thinking process.

First, take note of when you laugh and when you make others laugh. You will be surprised at how often you actually make other people laugh, and not just when you're dancing. It can be a great boost to your comedic ego to realize that you are truly a funny person. Whenever I conduct a workshop that is geared toward humor I ask the attendants how many think they are really funny. Almost no one raises their hands. Then I ask how often their friends laugh when they're together. Everyone raises their hand. Why is it we constantly make our friends laugh, but we don't think we're funny? What we need to do is recognize when and how we're funny and take note of our comedic personality.

We each have a comedic personality. An attitude that we take on when trying to make others laugh. Some are sarcastic, picking on everyone who innocently walks by the table. Some are dumbfounded, unable to understand the simplest things. Some are loud and bombastic, putting on the lampshade and dancing on the coffeetable. Take note of exactly what you say and do when others laugh at you. You don't have to try duplicating the same attitude for every occasion, but you will develop an awareness of your approach to humor.

Serious comedians always carry a small tape recorder with them. Not only is it used to tape their act in a comedy club for later evaluation and revision. They also use it to capture comedy ideas that come to them throughout the day. Try carrying one yourself, I'll bet if you recorded an entire night out with friends you would be amazed at how funny you are.

Part of learning is failure. And you must accept failure when learning comedy. It's tough when you fail at humor. When you're learning to play a new sport you accept that you are unskilled, so when you lose a game or look foolish on the court you pass it off to inexperience. When you're trying to be funny and you don't get a laugh, it's personal. It can also be embarrassing. Comedy is the most frightening thing to try (other than my mother's *Bouilla Baisse* fish head stew). Comedy is frightening because everyone, including you, knows if you fail. And your failure is far from private. The old axiom, *better to remain silent and be thought a fool than to open your mouth and remove all doubt,* prevents a lot of people from opening their mouths and trying comedy. The drawback is, they never get funny.

Find a safe environment and experiment. If you fail at getting laughs in front of close friends they'll just pass it off to you being off your medication. Be aware of how your make your friends laugh and bring your comedy attitude into new arenas in life. The risk will be worth it.

Chapter 19
WHAT'S NEXT IN COMEDY?

"Not to understand another man's purpose,
does not make <u>him</u> confused"
Confucius

(Okay, so I've got <u>one</u> quote that doesn't have anything to do with the book. It is still a cool quote.)

With what we now know of humor and its importance to the human condition, we must give comedy a more important seat in society. A civilization can not become so advanced technologically that it loses sight of its most important goal, the growth and fulfillment of each individual. One of the great killers of humor in America has been the corporate workplace. Someone long ago mistakenly decided that people can not be productive and happy at the same time, that professional demeanor and humor don't mix. These sour-pusses led us to believe that being funny in business was *inappropriate behavior* (being a comedian you can imagine how much I hate that phrase). This grew out of fear at the management level. When workers are laughing they feel alive. When they feel alive they feel in control. Many managers don't like the idea of a workforce that is in control—just look at contract negotiations between executives and labor unions. This way of must fall by the wayside if we are to avoid becoming an anthill society.

A look at Japanese villages, where members perform backbreaking work from dawn to bedtime every day and not tire, shows that good humor is the key to productivity and longevity. Teams of Japanese women plant rice seedlings in rows while singing at the top of their lungs. Men throw good-natured barbs at each other while hoisting bales and cutting wood.

almost any period or culture in which there is heavy labor you can find humor used to lighten the load. From the French voyageurs paddling heavy canoes upstream in 18th century Canada, to modern construction workers riveting steel girders on a skyscraper, good-natured joking keeps the work light. Humor builds spirit and creates a sense of community. When was the last time you felt a sense of community in the corporate boardroom while the big cheese flipped charts and talked about third quarter earnings? Probably when someone cracked a joke. Too bad everyone had to look to the boss to see if he laughed before they did.

The urge to own our own businesses comes not from a need to be our own boss. We start our own businesses so we can **be our own person.** That means having more fun. If we all had a blast every day at work we would never leave. We wouldn't want to miss the fun. Corporations and businesses need to realize that more humor in the workplace will reduce sickdays, absences, and employee turn-over. A positive atmosphere brought on by **daily laughter** improves productivity more than once-a-month training sessions or motivational pep talks.

Over the years I have conducted hundreds of seminars for businesses, corporations, and professional associations. The focus of my presentations is improvisational techniques for improved productivity. Every group I work with expects the typical presentation filled with flip-charts, graphs, and psycho-jargon. To their surprise they get none of that, instead we engage in hands-on exercises that foster a sense of play, a feeling of cooperation, and an atmosphere of **fun**. The exercises are challenging, but they are conducted in a way that emphasizes a no-winners, no-losers attitude. From the very start of the workshop there is laughter, but it's not because a speaker is telling amusing anecdotes. The people laugh together as they learn new skills and play. Each exercise has a specific technique that is to be learned, but each is to be "played," not "worked at." I have been told by participants at these seminars that they have much longer lasting effects that the typical speaker. They discover that if the techniques are practiced on a daily basis they produce positive changes in not only the individual, but in the attitude of the workplace as a whole.

Permission to laugh is given at the start of the workshop simply by creating an atmosphere where it's impossible not to laugh. Everyone has so much fun that they don't realize that they're performing difficult tasks. Quite a few managers and administrators have told me that they use some of the exercises at the start of every staff meeting. They have experienced a remarkable increase in creative ideas and teamwork. Laughter at the outset of a meeting helps transform the mood. A bonding occurs that can be achieved only through the positive chemistry of laughter.

CEOs, presidents, and managers need to recognize the most important condition of laughter, a light-hearted atmosphere in which laughter is permitted. They need to create an atmosphere in the workplace where the employees are not only given permission to laugh, but are encouraged to laugh. Managers should be trained in the area of humor. It is a skill, and like any other skill it requires practice. Proficiency in humor requires the ability to sense the mood of those around you. Comedy professionals are acutely aware of verbal and nonverbal signals that give feedback from the listener. A good comedian always is aware of the mood of the audience and can adjust accordingly. Imagine how much more effective managers would be in business if these attributes were part of their training.

Progressive companies are realizing that old management techniques and hierarchical systems no longer work. These companies are changing the structure of management. As positive as these changes are, the workplace needs to take one more step and change the way each individual is allowed to express him or herself through humor. Some companies have learned that if people are forced to be productive out of a fear losing their job they will do only what is required of them and look eagerly toward retirement. These companies have learned the value of freedom in the workplace, and nothing instills a sense of freedom more than laughter and a communal sense of fun.

At one company workshop I was confronted by an engineer who asked, "Why are we learning these techniques of interaction? We don't work with people, we work with machines." My response has become a cornerstone philosophy of mine, "No one works with machines. You work *on* machines, you work *with* people." The only reason you should get up everyday and drive through rush hour traffic to get to a job is because you like being there. The only reason you really like being anywhere is the feeling you get, feelings come from people, not calculators, computers, or toolboxes. Laughter makes us feel good about being where we are. Shouldn't it be the foundation of the workplace?

A change in society's views on humor must also extend into the family. A healthy family is one in which each member feels completely safe, unconditionally loved, and fully accepted. Many children are admonished for "acting up" and told to settle down, act their age, to take their work seriously. To take work seriously doesn't mean to be somber while doing it. Making work a game should be more than a trick to get children to do their homework, it should be a means of training children the techniques of creativity that will help them throughout life. Parents and teachers need to instill a sense of fun in their children that will carry on to the next generation.

Every person I know who loves spending time with their family describes their time together with the phrase, "We laugh all the time." It is funny that when we meet other families we find that their sense of humor is so unique to them that all they need is one word from each other and they will be on the floor holding their sides. We usually sit quietly wondering what the joke was about. No form of expression is so personal as a sense of humor. If a family can support each others attempts at comedy, even if the jokes are unsuccessful, the family will build a sense of security. That security will enable them to face challenges with confidence.

In recent years, schools in my area from 4th to 12th grade have requested talks about humor. These talks aren't to make the kids laugh and entertain them, they are to discuss the real basis of humor and how it affects our lives. The children are fascinated at what makes things funny. At very young ages they realize the power laughter possesses. To make your friends laugh is a very unique skill and bears understanding. The children also learn that laughter can be used to attack the wrong person or to make light of dangerous ideas or behavior. The opportunity to guide children's use of jokes and humor is an important role of a teacher and a parent.

In order to fully reap the benefits of laughter, humor must be supported in all areas of life. We must support those who take the risk to try for a laugh, and we must take the risk ourselves. Great leaders have all had a powerful sense of humor, not because they were particularly gifted comedians, but because they knew the value of living life fully. In almost any group with which I have contact–companies, organizations, clubs, or social gatherings–the leaders of the group are not chosen because they are the smartest. They are in charge because they let their natural personality shine through with confidence. We don't elect presidents and senators because we know anything about politics. We know very little about politics. We elect people because we like what we see. A person who can make a room full of people laugh exudes confidence. Nothing gives more power to a person than humor (besides an AK-47 assault rifle). People have said to me, "Well sure, Mr. Binkham can act all powerful and sure of himself, he's the president and CEO of the company." I say, "He got to be president *because* he's confident and has good humor."

When little kids play tag they are able to play for hours without stop. They are so focused on the game and having fun they never realize what time it is. After five hours of tag, mom or dad scream out the window, "Time for bed!" Kids always say, "But we just started!" When you have fun and laugh, there isn't a task at hand that doesn't fly by faster and with greater ease.

So, this is your challenge. Find where laughter can make your life better. Look for your opportunity to find and create laughter of delight. Start by listening for the laughs around you. Little children at play (no better sound in the world), young lovers in the park giggling at a private joke, two frat boys guffawing over beers, the melodic rise and fall of chuckling people gathered in the lunchroom, or a grandmother laughing with glee at the sight of a newborn baby in the family. Surprise yourself by laughing at a situation that you would normally curse. Remember, the result of surprise, frustration, and tension can be either laughter or anger. Substitution one for the other.

A friend of mine was siting with his little daughter. They were trying to decide what to do for fun. Finally she looked up at him and said, "Daddy. Let's laugh." So they just sat on the porch and laughed. Mom soon joined. Laugh, and the world... you know the rest.

"Laughter is the language of the soul."
Pablo Neruda

I first heard this quote on the animated comedy series, "The Simpsons." One of the greatest poets of the 20th century being quoted on a cartoon show, I can think of no better way to end this book.

Suggested Bathroom Reading

Books. Plays, and Publications

Bailey, John. Intent of Laughter. New York: New York Times Book Co., 1976.

Bergson, Henri. Laughter: An Essay on the Meaning of the Comic. New York:
    Macmillan Co., 1937.

Charney, Maurice. Comedy High and Low. New York: Oxford University Press, 1978.

Charney, Maurice. Comedy: New Perspectives, vol. 1. New York: New York Literary   Forum, 1978.

Corrigan, Robert W. Ed. Comedy: Meaning and Form. California: Chandler Publishing Co., 1965.

Durant, John, and Jonathan Miller. Laughing Matters: A Serious Look Humour. London: Longman Scientific & Technical., 1988.

Esslin, Martin. An Anatomy of Drama. New York: Hill and Wang, 1976.

Feibleman, James K. In Praise of Comedy. New York: Horizon Press, 1970.

Felheim, Marvin. Comedy: Plays, Theory and Criticism. New York: Harcourt Brace & World, Inc., 1962.

Freud, Sigmund. Jokes and Their Relation to the Unconscious. New York: Norton, 1960.

Gassner, John ed. A Treasury of the Theatre. New York: Simon and Schuster, 1967.

Gray, John, Ph.D. Men Are From Mars, Women Are From Venus. New York: HarperCollins, 1992.

Greig, John Young Thompson. The Psychology of Laughter and Comedy. New York: Cooper Square Publishers, Inc., 1969.

Grotjahn, Martin. Beyond Laughter. New York: Yale University Press, 1957.

Gurewitch, Morton. Comedy, The Irrational Vision. London: Cornell University Press, 1975.

Henderson, Jeffrey. The Maculate Muse. New York: Yale University Press, 1975.

Hogan, Robert and Sven Eric Molin. Drama: The Major Genres. New York: Dodd, Mead & Co., 1962.

Holland, Norman. Laughing, A Psychology of Humor. Ithaca: Cornell University Press, 1982.

Jackson, Holbrook. <u>Occasions</u>. New York: Simon and Schuster, 1969.

Johnson, Edgar. <u>A Treasury of Satire</u>. New York: Simon and Schuster, 1945.

Kerr, Walter. <u>Tragedy and Comedy</u>. New York: Simon and Schuster, 1967.

Legman, Gershon. <u>Rationale of the Dirty Joke</u>. New York: Grove Press, Inc., 1968.

Mamet, David. <u>Sexual Perversity in Chicago</u>. New York: Grove Press, 1974.

McCollom, William G. <u>The Divine Average</u>. Cleveland: Case Western Reserve, 1971.

Moliere, Jean. <u>Tartuffe</u>. Trans. Curtis Page, New York: The Knickerbocker Press, 1908.

Monro, David H. <u>Argument of Laughter</u>. Indiana: University of Notre Dame Press, 1963.

Paulos, John Allen. <u>Mathematics and Humor</u>. Chicago: University of Chicago Press, 1980.

Provine, Robert. <u>Laughter</u>. *American Scientist*, January, 1996

Rapp, Albert. <u>The Origins of Wit and Humor</u>. New York: E.P. Dutton & Co., Inc., 1951.

Swift, Jonathon. <u>Jonathon Swift and the Anatomy of Satire</u>. Ed. John M. Bullitt, Cambridge: Harvard University Press, 1961.

Thompson, Allen Reynolds. <u>The Anatomy of Drama</u>. 2nd ed. New York: Books for   Libraries Press, Inc., 1946.

Wilde, Oscar. <u>The Portable Oscar Wilde</u>. Ed. Richard Aldington, New York: The Viking   Press, 1947.

Recordings and Performances

Cosby, Bill. *Himself.* Motown Records, 1982.

Bruce, Lenny. *The Best of Lenny Bruce.* Fantasy Records.

Fiddler on the Roof.   Mirisch Production Company, United Artists

LA Story. Written by Steve Martin. Carolco Video, 1991

Newhart, Bob.   *The Button-Down Mind of Bob Newhart.* Warner Bros. Records, 1960.

Nichols, Mike, and Elaine May. *An Evening with Mike Nichols and Elaine May*.
Mercury Records, 1960.

Richard Pryor. *Bicentennial Nigger.* Warner Bros. Records, Inc., 1976.

Sherman, Allen. *My Son, the Folk Singer.* Warner Bros. Records, 1962.

Stiller, Jerry, and Anne Meara. *Ed Sullivan Presents: The Last Two People in the World.*
    Columbia Records.

The Ref. Written by Marie Weiss. Touchstone Pictures, 1994

Winters, Jonathan. *Jonathan Winters...Wings It!.* Columbia Records.

Index

I was going to have an index, but I wanted to list words like *the* and *to*. I thought it would be cool to have 10,000 listings for a preposition. The editors didn't think it was funny.

About the Author

Stephen "Stevie Ray" Rentfrow performed his first show at the age of nine. A comedy sketch with his two brothers at a family YMCA talent-night. Continuing to perform and study comedy, he designed his own college degree, *Theory and Performance of Comedy* at Moorhead State University in Minnesota.

He has toured the country as a solo comedian and with The Stevie Ray's Comedy Troupe. He has worked with such stars as Paula Poundstone, Marsha Warfield of "Night Court," and Rich Hall of "Saturday Night Live."

In 1989 he co-founded Stevie Ray's Productions with his partner Pamela Vervair. The company is focused on comedy performance and training, including improvisation, stand-up, sketches, music, and variety. He teaches at The School of Improv, conducts seminars at area schools, and is a guest faculty member of The Management Center, a division of The Graduate School of Business of the University of St. Thomas.

As a corporate trainer Stevie has traveled internationally, conducting *Improvisation for Professionals,* a program designed to teach employees the skills of improvisation to improve the workplace.

As a writer, Stevie's column, *Improvising Business,* appears regularly in the CityBusiness Newspaper of Minneapolis/St. Paul. His article, *Aiki-Improv,* comparing improvisation training to the martial arts, was published internationally in Aikido Today magazine.

A martial artist since 1977, he holds three black belts, with training in Goju-Ryu, Shotokan, Judo, Tae Kwon Do, Aikido, and weaponry. In the summer of 1983 he was Pee Wee Herman's bodyguard. He still lives by the philosophy, "I can run faster scared than you can mad."

An accomplished blues musician. He was nominated for Best Blues Harmonica Player in the 1988 Minnesota Blues Music Awards. He has opened for Jerry Portney and Matt "Guitar" Murphy of The Blues Brothers. After watching Stevie Ray play, Matt shook his hand and said, "Damn boy!" Either because Stevie was really good, or because he was standing on Matt's foot.

In his free time Stevie is a loving beekeeper and harvester of organic honey.

Stevie Ray's *"Making it up as we go since 1989"*